★ WHAT'S YOUR ★
GAY & LESBIAN
ENTERTAINMENT I.Q.?

Also by Ed Karvoski, Jr.

A Funny Time to Be Gay

WHAT'S YOUR
GAY & LESBIAN
ENTERTAINMENT I.Q.?

The Show-Biz Quiz About
What's "In" ... and
Who's "Out"

Ed Karvoski, Jr.

Kensington Books
http://www.kensingtonbooks.com

KENSINGTON BOOKS are published by

Kensington Publishing Corp.
850 Third Avenue
New York, NY 10022

First Kensington Printing: June, 1998
10 9 8 7 6 5 4 3 2 1

ISBN 1-57566-295-7

Printed in the United States of America

Dedicated to
Ma and Dad,
and Jay

Contents

☆ WHAT'S YOUR ☆
GAY & LESBIAN
ENTERTAINMENT I.Q.?

Introduction

"The world of entertainment is undergoing a revolution as homosexual culture enters the mainstream."

—*Entertainment Weekly*

What was the first image of a gay man, lesbian, or bisexual you saw in a feature film or television show? How about your all-time favorite? Or the portrayal you're most likely to induct into the Hall of Shame? Chances are they're all included between the covers of *What's Your Gay & Lesbian Entertainment I.Q.?*

What "out" performers and gay-friendly celebrities do you follow through the pages of *People, Us, Entertainment Weekly, Rolling Stone,* even *TV Guide*? They're covered here, too!

Learn for yourself exactly how much *you* know about gay/lesbian/bi-related films, television, theatre, and music. Grab a pen and charge up your "gaydar"! It's time to find out your *Gay & Lesbian Entertainment I.Q.*

Rating Scale

After answering all the questions, check the appropriate responses at the back of the book and add up your number of correct answers. The following rating scale will tell you your *Gay & Lesbian Entertainment I.Q.*

400 or More Correct Answers:

THE *VICTOR/VICTORIA* VICTORY AWARD

Congratulations! With your appreciation for diversity and eye for detail, you're the type of ardent fan who easily followed every complex twist of *Victor/Victoria*'s gender-bending plot line. (Perhaps if they had put Tom Cruise in drag, we all would have understood *Mission Impossible!*)

300–399 Correct Answers:

THE ELLEN DeGENERES "YEP, I'M GAY" AWARD

You don't have to be gay to receive this coveted honor. You qualify whether you're straight, bi, gay, a gay-wannabe, or you just aspire to be on the cover of *Time* magazine. As mentioned in *Ellen*'s coming-out episode, you deserve a cake that reads, GOOD FOR YOU—YOU'RE GAY!

200–299 Correct Answers:

THE RUPERT EVERETT "BEST FRIEND" AWARD

A spirited follower of gay-friendly entertainment, you stood up and sang along with Rupert Everett as you watched *My Best Friend's Wedding*. For that matter, you enthusiastically supported Melissa Etheridge, k.d. lang, and Elton John long before they announced they're friends of Dorothy's. Now *that's* what friends are for!

100–199 Correct Answers:

THE MARIEL HEMINGWAY *PERSONAL BEST* (BUT NO CIGAR) AWARD

You know what they say: It's not whether you win or lose, it's how you play the game—and keep playing till you eventually smooch with Roseanne on national television—that counts. Try, try again.

0–99 Correct Answers:

THE BAD DRAG SHOW AWARD

In this case, the word drag does not refer to the *festive* kind which has been masterfully performed by the likes of Patrick Swayze, Katharine Hepburn, Holly Woodlawn, and others too numerous (and *fabulous*) to list. Here, drag means—never mind, you wouldn't understand.

"Now At a Video Store Near You"

Circle the correct answer.

1. In *A Very Brady Sequel* (1996), who greets Carol Brady (Shelley Long) to Hawaii with the following information? "We're very open-minded here in the islands. In fact, you may have read about our liberal policies for gay people."
   (a) a flight attendant
   (b) a car rental clerk
   (c) a hotel concierge
   (d) Don Ho

2. In *Chasing Amy* (1997), Hooper (Dwight Ewell) is a cartoonist who is gay. What pair of cartoon characters does he insist are lovers?
   (a) Archie and Reggie
   (b) Archie and Jughead

(c) Reggie and Jughead

(d) Veronica and Betty

3. In *Leaving Normal* (1992), Darly (Christine Lahti) and Marianne (Meg Tilly) discuss the possibility of a boy growing up to be gay because of the way his mother . . .

(a) cuts his hair

(b) dresses him

(c) decorates his room

(d) breast-feeds him

4. What film did a reviewer for *Variety* describe as "Sexist, homophobic, and woefully unfunny to boot . . ."?

(a) *Robin Hood: Men in Tights* (1993), directed by Mel Brooks

(b) *Mo' Money* (1992), starring Damon Wayans

(c) *Bird on a Wire* (1990), starring Mel Gibson

(d) *Ladybugs* (1992), starring Rodney Dangerfield

5. In *Love! Valour! Compassion!* (1997, based on the stage play), Buzz (Jason Alexander) is referred to as "the love child of _____."

(a) Ethel Merman and Paul Lynde

(b) Judy Garland and Liberace

(c) Carol Channing and Charles Nelson Reilly

(d) k.d. lang and Harvey Fierstein

6. Also in *L! V! C!*, Buzz has a nightmare about a revival of *West Side Story* starring . . .

(a) Madonna and Antonio Banderas

(b) Robert Goulet and Cher

(c) Merv Griffin and Rosie O'Donnell

(d) John Travolta and Olivia Newton John

7. In *The First Wives Club* (1996), Brenda (Bette Midler), Elise (Goldie Hawn), and Annie (Diane Keaton) visit a lesbian bar. Brenda sits next to a crying woman and asks her what's wrong. Through tears, the woman responds, "It's my lover— she left me after 18 years for some teenager weighing _____ pounds!"
   (a) 2
   (b) 12
   (c) 120
   (d) 212

8. As the scene continues in *The First Wives Club*, Brenda tells the jilted lover, "Oh my God, that's just like me and Morty." Eying a photo of Morty, the crying woman remarks . . .
   (a) "She's cute."
   (b) "She's butch."
   (c) "She's available?"
   (d) "I think I dated her."

9. In what film does a group of Greek sailors in a bar sing the Village People's "Macho Man"?
   (a) *Wayne's World* (1992)
   (b) *Wayne's World 2* (1993)
   (c) *Addams Family Values* (1993)
   (d) *Police Academy* (1984)

10. In what film does a group of young straight guys in a bar sing the Village People's "Y.M.C.A."?
   (a) *Wayne's World*
   (b) *Wayne's World 2*
   (c) *Addams Family Values*
   (d) *Police Academy*

11. In the British film *Priest* (1994), Graham (Robert Carlyle)

takes Father Greg (Linus Roache) home with him. Following sex, Graham asks, "Are you_____? . . . It takes one to know one."

   (a) in the closet

   (b) bisexual

   (c) a Gemini

   (d) a Catholic

12. In *Threesome* (1994), Alex (Lara Flynn Boyle) performs in a lesbian production of . . .

   (a) *Macbeth*

   (b) *Oedipus Rex*

   (c) *Romeo and Juliet*

   (d) *The Odd Couple*

13. In *My Own Private Idaho* (1991), on what magazine cover does Scott (Keanu Reeves) appear as a model?

   (a) *Male Call*

   (b) *Joyboy*

   (c) *G-String*

   (d) *Butch*

14. Also in *My Own Private Idaho,* on what magazine cover does Mike (River Phoenix) appear as a model?

   (a) *Male Call*

   (b) *Joyboy*

   (c) *G-String*

   (d) *Butch*

15. What Arnold Schwarzenegger film includes a gay bar?

   (a) *Twins* (1988)

   (b) *Total Recall* (1990)

   (c) *True Lies* (1994)

   (d) *Erasure* (1996)

16. In what film does Madonna's character tell a jury that she left her former husband because he was in bed with another man?

(a) *Bloodhounds of Broadway* (1989)
(b) *Dick Tracy* (1990)
(c) *Body of Evidence* (1993)
(d) *Dangerous Game* (1994)

17. In *My Best Friend's Wedding* (1997), Julianne (Julia Roberts) and George (Rupert Everett), a gay man, are best friends. While pretending to be Julianne's fiancé, George leads a restaurant full of patrons in song. What song does he sing to her?

(a) "Wishin' and Hopin' "
(b) "The Way You Look Tonight"
(c) "I Say a Little Prayer"
(d) "What the World Needs Now Is Love"

Rupert Everett

18. Whoopi Goldberg plays a singer named Jane, who is a lesbian, in *Boys on the Side* (1995). In the film's opening scene, what Janis Joplin song does she sing?

   (a) "Bye, Bye, Baby"
   (b) "Piece of My Heart"
   (c) "Get It While You Can"
   (d) "Down on Me"

Boys on the Side

19. In *Bound* (1996), Violet (Jennifer Tilly) introduces herself and flirts with Corky (Gina Gershon), an ex-con who is a lesbian, by showing up at the door with . . .

   (a) coffee
   (b) beer
   (c) wine
   (d) flowers

20. How many years did Corky spend in jail?

   (a) 3
   (b) 4

(c) 5

(d) 6

21. Whose song plays over the closing credits of *Bound*?
   (a) Chaka Khan
   (b) Cyndi Lauper
   (c) Grace Jones
   (d) Tom Jones

22. Who is *not* included in the soundtrack of *To Wong Foo, Thanks for Everything, Julie Newmar* (1995)?
   (a) Chaka Khan
   (b) Cyndi Lauper
   (c) Grace Jones
   (d) Tom Jones

23. Who steps out of the shower in the opening scene of *To Wong Foo . . .*?
   (a) Patrick Swayze
   (b) Wesley Snipes
   (c) John Leguizamo
   (d) RuPaul

24. In a scene in *Private Resort* (1985), Ben (Rob Morrow from TV's *Northern Exposure*) is dressed in drag and gets groped from behind by two actors, Hector Elizondo and . . .
   (a) Johnny Depp
   (b) Robert Downey, Jr.
   (c) Luke Perry
   (d) Andrew Dice Clay

25. In *Six Degrees of Separation* (1993), Ouisa (Stockard Channing) watches Paul (Will Smith) in bed, naked, . . .
   (a) with a copy of *Honcho*

   (b) with a blow-up doll

   (c) with a hustler

   (d) saying his prayers

26. In *Flirting With Disaster* (1996), Nancy (Patricia Arquette) runs into Tony, an old classmate from high school who is now a police officer in Michigan. (Nancy soon discovers that he's bisexual.) In what city did they attend high school?

   (a) Chicago

   (b) Columbus

   (c) Detroit

   (d) Milwaukee

27. In *The Incredibly True Adventures of Two Girls in Love* (1995), Randy (Laurell Holloman) and Evie (Nicole Parker) are two teenagers who fall in love. What's the name of the high school they attend?

   (a) Wyman High

   (b) Wendell High

   (c) Wallace High

   (d) Washington High

28. Also in *Two Girls in Love,* Randy lives with her lesbian aunt, her aunt's lover, and her aunt's ex-lover. When Randy invites Evie to meet her family, what do they have for dinner?

   (a) whole-wheat pizza

   (b) organic pasta

   (c) tofu tacos

   (d) three-bean soup

29. In *Tombstone* (1993), Jason Priestly (from TV's *Beverly Hills 90210*) plays a gay cowboy, nicknamed . . .

   (a) Snowflake

   (b) Sister Boy

(c) Beach Boy

(d) Miss Muscle

30. In *The Wedding Banquet* (1993), while Wai Tung (Winston Chao) receives a visit from his parents, his lover Simon (Mitchell Lichtenstein) pretends to be his landlord. Simon asks, "How's my performance on the first day?" Wai Tung responds, "About a _____."

(a) A–

(b) B+

(c) B–

(d) C

31. In *In & Out* (1997), Cameron Drake (Matt Dillon) is an actor who wins an Oscar for his portrayal of a gay character. At the Academy Awards ceremony, who announces him the winner?

(a) Whoopi Goldberg

(b) Glenn Close

(c) Meryl Streep

(d) Billy Crystal

32. As the scene continues in *In & Out*, the Oscar-winning actor proclaims, "I'd like to dedicate this whole night to a great guy and a great teacher—to Howard Bracket from _____, Indiana . . . and he's gay."

(a) Greenfield

(b) Greenleaf

(c) Greentown

(d) Greenville

33. Also in *In & Out*, Howard (Kevin Kline), listens to an audio tape entitled "Exploring Your Masculinity: Getting a

Grip." The voice on the tape commands, "Above all else, do not dance." At that point, what song blares forth?

(a) "It's Raining Men"

(b) "I Need a Man"

(c) "Macho Man"

(d) "I Will Survive"

34. What cast member from *Love! Valour! Compassion!* also appears in *Lie Down With Dogs* (1995)?

(a) Randy Becker

(b) John Glover

(c) Stephen Spinella

(d) Jason Alexander

35. In *Lie Down With Dogs,* Tommie (Wally White) gets away from New York City and hitches a ride in a jeep with a pair of twins on their way to Provincetown. What are the names of the twins?

(a) Paul and Sam

(b) Peter and Sal

(c) Peter and Paul

(d) Sam and Sal

36. Also in *Lie Down With Dogs,* Guy (Bash Hollow) welcomes Tommie to Provincetown with the following information. "It's this town, you'll see. People here go through jobs like they go through _____."

(a) boyfriends

(b) Speedos

(c) condoms

(d) tanning lotion

37. An employment counselor in *Lie Down With Dogs* offers the following tips. "Be sexy, be smart, and be _____."

(a) well dressed

(b) clean-cut
(c) on time
(d) festive

38. In *Kiss Me, Guido* (1997), Terry (Craig Chester) tries to help his friend Warren (Anthony Barrile) by secretly placing an ad seeking a "gay, white male" for an apartment to share. Where does he place the ad?
   (a) *The New York Times*
   (b) *The New York Post*
   (c) *The Village Voice*
   (d) *Homo X-tra*

39. Frankie (Nick Scotti), a straight man who answers the ad in *Kiss Me, Guido,* works at a pizza parlor in . . .
   (a) Queens
   (b) Brooklyn
   (c) the Bronx
   (d) Staten Island

40. Also in *Kiss Me, Guido,* Frankie thinks GWM (Gay, White Male) stands for Guy With _____.
   (a) Morals
   (b) Money
   (c) Mongrel
   (d) Meaning

41. Craig Chester co-stars in *Swoon* (1992), based on the 1924 murder case involving lovers Richard "Dickie" Loeb and Nathan "Babe" Leopold, Jr. Which one of the couple does Chester portray?
   (a) Richard Loeb
   (b) Nathan Leopold, Jr.

42. In what film does Goldie Hawn play a character whose roommates are a gay couple?
   (a) *The First Wives Club* (1996)
   (b) *Bird on a Wire* (1990)
   (c) *Overboard* (1987)
   (d) *Protocol* (1984)

43. In what film do students form a nondiscriminating fraternity called Lambda Lambda Lambda?
   (a) *Back to School* (1986)
   (b) *Threesome* (1994)
   (c) *Revenge of the Nerds* (1984)
   (d) *PCU* (1994)

44. In *The Brady Bunch Movie* (1995), a teenage girl has a crush on . . .
   (a) Marcia
   (b) Jan
   (c) Cindy
   (d) Alice

45. What is the name of that teenage girl in *The Brady Bunch Movie?*
   (a) Dora
   (b) Doreen
   (c) Noreen
   (d) Nora

46. In *Little Darlings* (1980), whose character is suspected of being a lesbian by the other girls at summer camp and must lose her virginity to prove them wrong?
   (a) Mary Stuart Masterson

   (b) Mary-Louise Parker
   (c) Jodie Foster
   (d) Kristy McNichol

47. In *Jeffrey* (1995, based on the stage play), Robert Klein plays the host of a game show called . . .
   (a) *What's My Sex?*
   (b) *Name That Sex*
   (c) *It's Just Sex*
   (d) *Wheel of Foreskin*

48. Who makes a cameo appearance in *Jeffrey* as a TV reporter?
   (a) Dennis Miller
   (b) Kevin Nealon
   (c) Phil Hartman
   (d) Simon Rex

49. Also in *Jeffrey*, Nathan Lane's character states, "I'm a Catholic priest. Historically, that falls between chorus boy and _____."
   (a) hairdresser
   (b) interior decorator
   (c) florist
   (d) film critic

50. In *Three of Hearts* (1993), who portrays a male escort who is hired by a lesbian to go out with her ex-girlfriend?
   (a) Alec Baldwin
   (b) James Baldwin
   (c) Stephen Baldwin
   (d) William Baldwin

51. The advertising tag line for *Bar Girls* (1994, based on

the stage play) read, "Finally, a romantic comedy without _____."
   (a) incorrect politics
   (b) high heels
   (c) men
   (d) a Baldwin brother

52. Chastity Bono makes a cameo appearance as a bar patron in *Bar Girls*. What is her character's astrological sign?
   (a) Taurus
   (b) Gemini
   (c) Scorpio
   (d) Sagittarius

53. In *Torch Song Trilogy* (1988, based on the stage play), Ed (Brian Kerwin) meets Arnold (Harvey Fierstein) in a bar and shares his astrological sign. What is Ed's sign?
   (a) Taurus
   (b) Gemini
   (c) Scorpio
   (d) Sagittarius

54. In Spike Lee's *Get On The Bus* (1996), Randall (Harry Lennix) and Kyle (Isaiah Washington) are gay men on their way to the Million Man March in Washington, D.C. What book is Kyle seen reading?
   (a) *B-Boy Blues*
   (b) *The Color Purple*
   (c) *Invisible Life*
   (d) *Queer in America*

55. In the British film *My Beautiful Launderette* (1985), Johnny (Daniel Day-Lewis) and Omar (Gordon Warnecke) become

lovers and business partners as they spruce up a launderette and name it . . .

(a) Suds
(b) Bubbles
(c) Poofters
(d) Powders

56. What was the former name of the business in *My Beautiful Launderette?*

(a) Windsor's Launderette
(b) Buckingham's Launderette
(c) Churchill's Launderette
(d) The Queen's Launderette

57. In a scene in *It's My Party* (1996), while Nick (Eric Roberts) and Brandon (Gregory Harrison) are in bed together, what Woody Allen film are they watching?

(a) *Annie Hall*
(b) *Love and Death*
(c) *Manhattan*
(d) *Everything You Always Wanted to Know About Sex*

58. Also in *It's My Party,* Monty (Bronson Pinchot) eyes a jacket worn by Damian (Roddy McDowall) and remarks, ''My mother has _____ in that fabric.''

(a) a housedress
(b) a toaster cozy
(c) sofa upholstery
(d) drapes

59. In a scene in *National Lampoon's Loaded Weapon 1* (1992), Emilio Estevez is seen wearing . . .

(a) black leather chaps
(b) red lingerie

(c) a Carmen Miranda costume

(d) a "Mighty Dykes" T-shirt

60. In *My Fellow Americans* (1996), two former presidents, President Kramer (James Garner) and President Douglas (Jack Lemmon), unknowingly step into the middle of a gay pride march. The celebration includes a marching band with all of its members dressed like a character from *The Wizard of Oz*. Which character?

(a) Scarecrow

(b) Tin Man

(c) Cowardly Lion

(d) Dorothy

61. One of the gay pride marchers gives President Douglas . . .

(a) a rainbow flag

(b) a pink triangle

(c) a freedom-ring necklace

(d) a kiss

62. In what state is the gay pride march in *My Fellow Americans*?

(a) Ohio

(b) West Virginia

(c) Virginia

(d) Kansas

63. In *Mrs. Doubtfire* (1993), Daniel (Robin Williams) enlists the aid of his brother Frank (Harvey Fierstein), a makeup artist who is gay. "It's a busy life," declares Frank. "Places to go, _____."

(a) faces to paint

(b) lips to gloss
(c) eyebrows to tweeze
(d) beards to hot wax

64. Fierstein's character in *Mrs. Doubtfire* is referred to as Uncle Frank. Scott Capurro plays his partner, referred to as . . .

(a) Uncle Jason
(b) Uncle Justin
(c) Uncle Jack
(d) Aunt Jack

65. In Woody Allen's *Bullets Over Broadway* (1994), Harvey Fierstein appears in a small role as . . .

(a) an actor
(b) an agent
(c) a playwright
(d) a choreographer

66. James Coco received an Academy Award nomination for Best Supporting Actor for his portrayal of Jimmy, a gay man, in Neil Simon's *Only When I Laugh* (1981). The character is a failed . . .

(a) actor
(b) agent
(c) playwright
(d) choreographer

67. William Hurt won an Oscar for Best Actor for *Kiss of the Spider Woman* (1985), becoming the first actor to win the award for playing a gay role. The film also received three other nominations. For which of the following awards was the film *not* nominated?

(a) Best Actress
(b) Best Screenplay

(c) Best Director

(d) Best Picture

68. In *Mannequin* (1987), Meshach Taylor plays a flamboyant window dresser named . . .

(a) Miami

(b) Castro

(c) Hollywood

(d) West Hollywood

69. Also in *Mannequin,* Meshach Taylor's character drives a pink Cadillac with licence plates that read . . .

(a) GOOD BOY

(b) BAD BOY

(c) GOOD GIRL

(d) BAD GIRL

70. In *Honky Tonk Freeway* (1981), four gay guys are seen in a jeep with a bumper sticker that reads, "_____."

(a) HONK IF YOU'RE HORNY

(b) I'D RATHER BE SHOPPING

(c) NOBODY KNOWS I'M GAY

(d) BUT CHA ARE, BLANCHE

71. In *The World According to Garp* (1982), Roberta (John Lithgow) underwent a sex-change operation. Roberta was formerly a tight end with the . . .

(a) Philadelphia Eagles

(b) New York Jets

(c) Los Angeles Raiders

(d) San Francisco 49ers

The World According to Garp

72. In *The Brady Bunch Movie,* drag star RuPaul plays a guidance counselor named Mrs. Cummings. Which one of the Brady kids visits Mrs. Cummings for advice?
  (a) Peter
  (b) Jan
  (c) Greg
  (d) Marcia

73. What is the opening song in *The Adventures of Priscilla, Queen of the Desert* (1994)?
  (a) "Mama Mia"
  (b) "I Will Survive"
  (c) "I Love The Nightlife"
  (d) "I've Never Been to Me"

RuPaul

74. What is the opening song in *The Birdcage* (1996, based on the 1979 French film *La Cage aux Folles*)?
   (a) "Conga"
   (b) "She Works Hard for The Money"
   (c) "We Are Family"
   (d) "Can That Boy Fox Trot"

75. In a scene in *The Birdcage,* Agador (Hank Azaria) is seen wearing a T-shirt that reads . . .
   (a) STRAIGHT ACTING
   (b) STRAIGHT LOOKING
   (c) STRAIGHTS WELCOMED
   (d) I CAN'T EVEN THINK STRAIGHT

76. In the British film *Alive & Kicking* (1997), Tonio (Jason Flemyng), a gay man who is HIV-positive, is on the dance floor at a club and swaps his T-shirt with another dancer. Tonio receives a _____ T-shirt.
   (a) Superman
   (b) Hercules
   (c) George of the Jungle
   (d) Mr. Bubble

77. In another scene in *Alive & Kicking*, while Tonio is rehearsing a dance piece, he is seen wearing a T-shirt that reads . . .
   (a) DIVA
   (b) PRIMA DONNA
   (c) BALLERINA BABE
   (d) PSYCHO BITCH

78. In the opening scene of *Bar Girls*, Loretta (Nancy Allison Wolfe) is preparing to go out for the evening. Among the many outfits she tries and rejects is a T-shirt that reads . . .
   (a) I'M NOT GAY BUT MY GIRLFRIEND IS
   (b) TIGHT BUTTS DRIVE ME NUTS
   (c) SIT ON A HAPPY FACE
   (d) DRAMA DYKE

79. Also in *Bar Girls*, Loretta says to Rachael (Liza D'Adostino), "Let's try not to get too analytical on our first meeting, or we may cancel ourselves out before we even get to decide who gets the _____ when we break up."
   (a) cats
   (b) furniture
   (c) apartment
   (d) Rita Mae Brown books

80. In *Six Degrees of Separation,* Trent (Anthony Michael Hall) recounts his initial attraction to Paul (Will Smith), recalling that they met on the street, then went home together. What was the weather condition when they met?
  (a) windy
  (b) raining
  (c) snowing
  (d) a heat wave

81. In what film does a clerk at an Army surplus store scream the following jeer at two gay customers?
"Alternative lifestyle my ass!"
  (a) *Crocodile Dundee* (1986)
  (b) *Crocodile Dundee II* (1988)
  (c) *Zorro, the Gay Blade* (1981)
  (d) *Falling Down* (1993)

82. In what film does a man who is about to jump from a window ledge say, "I loved that bitch, and he betrayed me!"?
  (a) *Crocodile Dundee*
  (b) *Crocodile Dundee II*
  (c) *Zorro, the Gay Blade*
  (d) *Falling Down*

83. In *The Hunger* (1983), Catherine Deneuve plays a bisexual vampire. Who plays her vampire husband?
  (a) Mick Jagger
  (b) George Michaels
  (c) Sting
  (d) David Bowie

84. Who plays a lisping, limp-wristed camp lieutenant in *Meatballs Part II* (1984)?
  (a) Bill Murray

(b) John Larroquette
(c) Richard Mulligan
(d) Ted Danson

85. In *Go Fish* (1994), Max (Guinevere Turner) concedes that her real name is . . .
   (a) Camille
   (b) Gertrude
   (c) Guinevere
   (d) Margaret

Guinevere Turner

86. John Ritter plays Vaughan, a gay man, in *Sling Blade* (1996). What is Vaughan's boyfriend's name?
   (a) Albert
   (b) Gilbert
   (c) Hubert
   (d) Robert

87. In *The Wedding Banquet,* what's the name of the restaurant where the wedding banquet takes place?
   (a) The China Bowl
   (b) The China Palace
   (c) The China Garden
   (d) The China Blossom

88. What is the number of the honeymoon suite in *The Wedding Banquet?*
   (a) 1040
   (b) 1069
   (c) 1080
   (d) 5050

89. In *Alive & Kicking,* Jack (Antony Sher) is an AIDS counselor who becomes Tonio's (Jason Flemyng) lover. What is Jack's apartment number?
   (a) 2
   (b) 4
   (c) 6
   (d) 8

90. In *Threesome,* what is the number of the dorm suite shared by Eddy (Josh Charles), Stuart (Stephen Baldwin), and Alex (Lara Flynn Boyle)?
   (a) 3
   (b) 3S

(c) 3D

(d) 3X

91. Also in *Threesome,* Eddy, Stuart, and Alex rent a convertible from a business called . . .

(a) Rent-A-Heap

(b) Rent-A-Junk

(c) Rent-A-Wreck

(d) Rent-A-Clunker

92. Who plays a gay next-door neighbor in *The Prince of Tides* (1991)?

(a) Robert Klein

(b) Kevin Kline

(c) George Carlin

(d) George Clooney

93. Who plays a gay next-door neighbor in *Frankie & Johnny* (1991, based on the stage play *Frankie and Johnny in the Clair de Lune)?*

(a) Jason Alexander

(b) Jason Patric

(c) Patrick Cassidy

(d) Nathan Lane

94. The advertising tag line for *The Adventures of Priscilla, Queen of the Desert* read, ''Finally, a comedy that will change the way you think, the way you feel, and most important, the way you _____.''

(a) dress

(b) accessorize

(c) travel

(d) lip-synch

95. The advertising tag line for *To Wong Foo* . . . read, "_____ is everything."
   (a) Mascara
   (b) Lip gloss
   (c) Attitude
   (d) A sense of direction

96. What film proclaimed the following advertising tag line? "In a world that expects you to fit in, sometimes you have to stand out."
   (a) *Go Fish* (1994)
   (b) *All Over Me* (1997)
   (c) *Beautiful Thing* (1996)
   (d) *The Incredibly True Adventures of Two Girls in Love* (1995)

97. In *Serial* (1980), a shrink gives a 10-year-old boy a _____ doll.
   (a) Barbie
   (b) Ken
   (c) G.I. Joe
   (d) Gay Bruce

98. In *Home for the Holidays* (1995), Robert Downey, Jr., plays a gay member of a dysfunctional family. Who directed the film?
   (a) Gus Van Sant
   (b) Gregg Araki
   (c) Pedro Almodovar
   (d) Jodie Foster

99. In the 1983 remake of *To Be Or Not to Be,* Sasha (James "Gypsy" Haake) is identified as a homosexual by the Nazis and is forced to wear a pink triangle. "I hate it," he says, referring to the pink triangle. "It clashes with _____."
   (a) my eyes

(b) my rouge

(c) my pearls

(d) everything

100. Who plays the daughter of drag star Divine in *Hairspray* (1988)?

(a) Pia Zadora

(b) Deborah Harry

(c) Ricki Lake

(d) Sally Jessy Raphael

101. In *Sunset* (1988), written and directed by Blake Edwards, who plays a character who operates a brothel and pretends to be a lesbian to detract customers?

(a) Lesley Ann Warren

(b) Kathleen Quinlan

(c) Mariel Hemingway

(d) Julie Andrews

102. In *Garbo Talks* (1984), Harvey Fierstein plays a gay man who is vacationing . . .

(a) in San Francisco

(b) in Miami

(c) in Key West

(d) on Fire Island

103. In *Polyester* (1981), directed by John Waters, Tab Hunter plays a character named . . .

(a) Todd Yesterday

(b) Todd Today

(c) Todd Tomorrow

(d) Todd Sweeney

104. *Common Threads: Stories from the Quilt,* the 1989 Academy

Award winner for Best Documentary, focuses on five individuals with AIDS. Who narrated the documentary?

  (a) Dustin Hoffman

  (b) Al Pacino

  (c) Meryl Streep

  (d) Lily Tomlin

105. In *Four Weddings and a Funeral* (1994), Gareth (Simon Callow) and Matthew (John Hannah) are lovers. In the opening montage, as they get ready to attend a wedding, which one of the couple is seen preparing breakfast?

  (a) Gareth

  (b) Matthew

106. Also in *Four Weddings and a Funeral,* Fiona (Kristin Scott Thomas) confides to a reception guest, "I was a lesbian once at school, but only for about _____ minutes. I don't think it counts."

  (a) 5

  (b) 10

  (c) 15

  (d) 20

107. Who portrays a flamboyant columnist in the British film *Evil Under the Sun* (1982), based on the Agatha Christie novel?

  (a) Anthony Perkins

  (b) Roddy McDowall

  (c) Robert Morse

  (d) Charles Nelson Reilly

108. The British film *Beautiful Thing* (1996, based on the stage play) focuses on the story of a gay teenage couple. The

cast of characters also includes a Jamaican girl who is obsessed with singer . . .

  (a) Dusty Springfield
  (b) Dionne Warwick
  (c) Mama Cass
  (d) Lulu

109. In *Desert Hearts* (1985), Vivian (Helen Shaver) goes to Reno in the 1950s to get a divorce and examines her sexuality. How many years was she married to her husband?

  (a) 11
  (b) 12
  (c) 13
  (d) 14

110. Queen Latifah plays Cleo, a lesbian, in *Set It Off* (1996). In addition to robbing banks, Cleo and her cohorts work for an office-cleaning business called _____ Janitorial.

  (a) Leon's
  (b) Larry's
  (c) Lionel's
  (d) Luther's

111. Also in *Set It Off*, a friend notes to Cleo that she's been fixing up her Chevy Impala since _____ grade.

  (a) 5th
  (b) 6th
  (c) 7th
  (d) 8th

112. In the German film *Querelle* (1982), Brad Davis portrays a gay . . .

  (a) sailor
  (b) soldier

(c) cop

(d) construction worker

113. In *Can't Stop the Music* (1980), Ray, one of the Village People, appears as a . . .

(a) sailor

(b) soldier

(c) cop

(d) construction worker

2

Celluloid Scrapbook

Circle the correct answer.

114. Who made her film debut by playing a lesbian in *The Group* (1966)?
   (a) Catherine Deneuve
   (b) Candice Bergen
   (c) Glenda Jackson
   (d) Divine

115. In what film does Woody Allen muse, "I wonder if Socrates and Plato took a house on Crete during the summer?"?
   (a) *Annie Hall* (1977)
   (b) *Love and Death* (1975)
   (c) *Manhattan* (1979)
   (d) *Everything You Always Wanted to Know About Sex (But Were Afraid to Ask)* (1972)

116. Who portrays a fag hag in *Some of My Best Friends Are . . .* (1971)?
   (a) Bea Arthur
   (b) Betty White
   (c) Rue McClanahan
   (d) Estelle Getty

117. In *The Ritz* (1976, based on the stage play), who plays a straight detective in a gay bathhouse, wearing only a towel throughout the movie?
   (a) William Hurt
   (b) William Baldwin
   (c) Treat Williams
   (d) Robin Williams

118. Also in *The Ritz,* who portrays a cabaret singer who performs at the gay bathhouse?
   (a) Bette Midler
   (b) Chita Rivera
   (c) Rita Moreno
   (d) Charles Pierce

119. In what Barbra Streisand film does Viveca Lindfors play a lesbian?
   (a) *Up on the Sandbox* (1972)
   (b) *The Way We Were* (1973)
   (c) *For Pete's Sake* (1974)
   (d) *Funny Lady* (1975)

120. Actress June Allyson (known to a new generation for her TV commercials for Depends) was told to report to work on *They Only Shoot Their Masters* (1972) dressed as a lesbian. What did she show up wearing?
   (a) her father's tuxedo

(b) her husband's army fatigues

(c) her son's football sweatshirt

(d) a nun's habit

121. In *Advise and Consent* (1962), Don Murray plays a U.S. senator who receives anonymous calls threatening to expose him as a homosexual who was involved with a man while in . . .

(a) prep school

(b) the Navy

(c) the Olympics

(d) Key West

122. Also in *Advise and Consent,* what singer is heard from the juke box in a gay bar?

(a) Judy Garland

(b) Peggy Lee

(c) Billie Holiday

(d) Frank Sinatra

123. In *10* (1979), Dudley Moore plays George, a songwriter whose writing partner, Hugh, is gay. George refers to Hugh's friends as "the Malibu chapter of _____."

(a) the friends of Dorothy

(b) the Fruit Loop group

(c) the brunch bunch

(d) the sugarplum fairies

124. In *Just a Gigolo* (1979), who portrays a war vet who is pursued by both men and women?

(a) Richard Gere

(b) Mick Jagger

(c) David Bowie

(d) Marlene Dietrich

125. What film includes a gay robot?
   (a) *The Rocky Horror Picture Show* (1975)
   (b) *Flesh Gordon* (1974)
   (c) *Barbarella* (1968)
   (d) *Sleeper* (1973)

Barbara Stanwyck

126. In *The Balcony* (1963), Shelley Winters plays Miss Erma, a lesbian who is the proprietor of . . .

    (a) a drag bar in Greenwich Village

    (b) a women's health spa in Palm Springs

    (c) a bowling alley in New Jersey

    (d) a brothel in New Orleans

127. In *Walk on the Wild Side* (1962), Barbara Stanwyck plays Jo, a lesbian who is the proprietor of . . .

    (a) a drag bar in Greenwich Village

    (b) a women's health spa in Palm Springs

    (c) a bowling alley in New Jersey

    (d) a brothel in New Orleans

128. The advertising tag line for *The Gay Deceivers* (1969) read, "Wear long hair, tight-fitting pants, lisp a little, put your hands on your hips, quote liberally from Oscar Wilde and Marcel Proust, and ask your sergeant if he likes _____. You have nothing to lose but your draft card."

    (a) your uniform

    (b) your mascara

    (c) your flawlessly decorated barracks

    (d) your bunk bed or his

129. Lauded by critics as "the saving grace" of *The Gay Deceivers,* comic-actor Michael Greer portrays "a lovable stereotype" named Malcolm DeJohn. In the film, the character quips, "When Craig and I were first married, I didn't know a thing about cooking either. I used to dress a turkey in _____ _____."

    (a) leather

    (b) lace

    (c) lamé

    (d) Levi's

Michael Greer

130. Shelley Winters portrays Ma Parker in *Bloody Mary* (1970). Who plays her gay son?

   (a) Bruce Dern

   (b) Robert DeNiro

   (c) Robert Carradine

   (d) Jon Voight

131. In what film does Stella Stevens play a dope-dealing lesbian?

   (a) *Girls! Girls! Girls!* (1962)

   (b) *Advance to the Rear* (1964)

   (c) *The Silencer* (1966)

   (d) *Cleopatra Jones and the Casino of Gold* (1975)

132. In *Staircase* (1962), Richard Burton and Rex Harrison play unhappy homosexuals who are . . .

   (a) hairstylists

   (b) florists

   (c) interior decorators

   (d) film critics

133. What was the title of an experimental sound film at the Thomas Edison Studio in 1895 which showed two men dancing a waltz?

   (a) *The Gay Sisters*

   (b) *The Gay Brothers*

   (c) *The Cherry Sisters*

   (d) *The Pansy Brothers*

134. In *She Done Him Wrong* (1933), Mae West spots two prisoners in a jail cell with their arms around each other. What does she call them?

   (a) the Gay Sisters

   (b) the Gay Brothers

   (c) the Cherry Sisters

   (d) the Pansy Brothers

135. In *Tell Me That You Love Me, Julie Moon* (1970), a gay man meets a bodybuilder and names him . . .

   (a) Snowflake

   (b) Sister Boy

(c) Beach Boy
(d) Miss Muscle

136. Who portrays Hildegarde, a lesbian, in the Agatha Christie adaptation *Murder on the Orient Express* (1974)?
   (a) Jacqueline Bisset
   (b) Lauren Bacall
   (c) Rachel Roberts
   (d) Vanessa Redgrave

137. In *The Eiger Sanction* (1974), Jack Cassidy plays a gay man with a dog named . . .
   (a) Fifi
   (b) Froufrou
   (c) Fruity
   (d) Faggot

138. What film was described by reviewer Judith Crist in the following way? "If the gay-lib movement wants its own mediocre movie preachment—here it is."
   (a) *Boys in the Band* (1970)
   (b) *Dog Day Afternoon* (1975)
   (c) *A Very Natural Thing* (1973)
   (d) *Norman, Is That You?* (1976)

139. In *The Soilers* (1923), a silent film starring Laurel & Hardy, a gay cowboy blows a kiss to Stan Laurel and mouths . . .
   (a) "My hero!"
   (b) "My cowboy!"
   (c) "My, you look handsome in chaps!"
   (d) "My bunkhouse or yours?"

140. In the Fred Astaire-Ginger Rogers musical *The Gay Divorcee* (1934), Edward Everett plays a sissy named . . .

(a) Precious
(b) Prissy
(c) Pinky
(d) Mr. Joyboy

141. In *The Loved One* (1965), Rod Steiger plays a flamboyant mortuary cosmetician named . . .
(a) Precious
(b) Prissy
(c) Pinky
(d) Mr. Joyboy

142. Ray Walston (from TV's *My Favorite Martian*) plays an effeminate cosmetician in *Caprice* (1967). Whose character pushes him to his death from a balcony?
(a) Elizabeth Montgomery
(b) Elizabeth Taylor
(c) Debbie Reynolds
(d) Doris Day

143. In *The Boys in the Band* (1970), Michael (Kenneth Nelson) asks, "What's more boring than a queen doing a Judy Garland imitation?" Donald (Frederick Combs) responds, "A queen doing a _____ imitation."
(a) Mae West
(b) Bette Davis
(c) Carol Channing
(d) Glenda the Good Witch

Film Quotes

Who delivered the following lines, and in what films? Circle the correct answer.

144. "I truly believe that if we can get two women on the Supreme Court, we can get at least one for you."
    (a) Stephen Baldwin to Josh Charles in *Threesome* (1994)
    (b) Whoopi Goldberg to James Remar in *Boys on the Side* (1995)
    (c) Janeane Garofalo to Steve Zahn in *Reality Bites* (1994)

145. "I will find a substitute for sex—Sex Light . . . Sex Helper . . . I Can't Believe It's Not Sex."
    (a) Bronson Pinchot in *It's My Party* (1996)
    (b) Wally White in *Lie Down With Dogs* (1995)
    (c) Steven Weber in *Jeffrey* (1995)

146. "I don't have luck with women."
    (a) Uma Thurman in *Henry & June* (1990)
    (b) Sharon Stone in *Basic Instinct* (1992)
    (c) Ben Affleck in *Chasing Amy* (1997)

147. "Everybody likes to make themselves out to be something more than they are, especially in the homosexual underworld."
    (a) Kevin Bacon in *JFK* (1991)
    (b) Will Smith in *Six Degrees of Separation* (1993)
    (c) Craig Chester in *Swoon* (1992)

148. "They do that now, don't they? Call themselves lesbos. And she makes it sound like a compliment."
    (a) Diane Keaton in *The First Wives Club* (1996)
    (b) Anita Gilette in *Boys on the Side* (1995)
    (c) Jason Lee in *Chasing Amy* (1997)

149. "I walked into my room and there's a woman in my bed . . . And I thought, what the hell, let's try it once with a woman and see what those straight guys are raving about."
    (a) Winston Chao in *The Wedding Banquet* (1993)
    (b) Russell Crow in *The Sum of Us* (1994)
    (c) Robin Williams in *The Birdcage* (1996)

150. "It's not as if I'm gay. I'm just curious."
    (a) Ralph Macchio in *Naked in New York* (1994)
    (b) Stephen Lang in *Last Exit to Brooklyn* (1989)
    (c) Michael Ontkean in *Making Love* (1982)

151. "Look at me. Do I look like a homosexual?"
    (a) Kevin Kline in *In & Out* (1997)
    (b) Nick Scotti in *Kiss Me, Guido* (1997)
    (c) George Hamilton in *Zorro, the Gay Blade* (1981)

152. "What's wrong with these people? Don't they enjoy tantrums anymore?"
   (a) Jason Flemyng in *Alive & Kicking* (1997)
   (b) Jason Alexander in *Love! Valour! Compassion!* (1997)
   (c) Eric Roberts in *It's My Party* (1996)

153. "Honey, I'm more man than you'll ever be, and more woman than you'll ever get!"
   (a) Antonio Fargas in *Car Wash* (1976)
   (b) Meshach Taylor in *Mannequin* (1987)
   (c) Queen Latifah in *Set It Off* (1996)

154. "There are just some men who are very devoted to their mothers. You know, the type that likes to collect cooking recipes, exchange bits of gossip."
   (a) Rock Hudson to Doris Day in *Pillow Talk* (1959)
   (b) Rock Hudson to Doris Day in *Lover Come Back* (1961)
   (c) Rock Hudson to James Dean and Sal Mineo in *Giant* (1956)

155. "Just once I'd like to see a bisexual that lived with his boyfriend and then snuck out to see his girlfriend on the side!"
   (a) Christopher Guest in *Beyond Therapy* (1987)
   (b) Charles Pierce in *Torch Song Trilogy* (1988)
   (c) Harry Hamlin in *Making Love* (1982)

156. "You ran away femme and came back a big ol' butch."
   (a) Gina Gershon to Jennifer Tilly in *Bound* (1996)
   (b) Guinevere Turner to V.S. Brodie in *Go Fish* (1994)
   (c) Bridget Fonda to Peter Friedman in *Single White Female* (1992)

157. "I don't do fags."
    (a) Bruce Jenner in *Can't Stop the Music* (1980)
    (b) Angie Dickinson in *Dressed to Kill* (1980)
    (c) Richard Gere in *American Gigolo* (1980)

158. "Look, I don't have anything against homos. I mean, you are what you are, right? And it's okay if you look at my butt. It's a nice butt."
    (a) Eric Stoltz to Ralph Macchio in *Naked in New York* (1994)
    (b) Stephen Baldwin to Josh Charles in *Threesome* (1994)
    (c) Nick Scotti to Anthony Barrile in *Kiss Me, Guido* (1997)

159. "Nothing in this house is inappropriate."
    (a) Olympia Dukakis in *Tales of the City* (1993)
    (b) Jack Thompson in *The Sum of Us* (1994)
    (c) Lily Tomlin in *Flirting With Disaster* (1996)

160. "At least I have sense enough to know that racism and homophobia still exist."
    (a) Randy Becker in *Love! Valour! Compassion!* (1997)
    (b) Isaiah Washington in *Get on the Bus* (1996)
    (c) Denzel Washington in *Philadelphia* (1993)

161. "He lives with another guy and they both have great bodies. You tell me."
    (a) Margaret Cho in *It's My Party* (1996)
    (b) Mary-Louise Parker in *Longtime Companion* (1990)
    (c) Dwight Ewell in *Chasing Amy* (1997)

162. "I can be butch when I have to—I get it from my mother."
    (a) Jason Gould in *The Prince of Tides* (1991)
    (b) Liza Minnelli in *That's Entertainment!* (1974)
    (c) Peter Friedman in *Single White Female* (1992)

163. "I'm a lesbian, but that's not the issue here."
   (a) Cher in *Silkwood* (1983)
   (b) Jennifer Dundas in *The First Wives Club* (1996)
   (c) Swoosie Kurtz in *Citizen Ruth* (1996)

164. "If you think I'm worried about everyone thinking I'm a fag, you're right."
   (a) James Garner in *Victor/Victoria* (1982)
   (b) James Garner in *The Children's Hour* (1962)
   (c) James Garner in *My Fellow Americans* (1996)

165. "I think heterosexuality is gonna make a comeback."
   (a) Jason Lee in *Chasing Amy* (1997)
   (b) James Remar in *Boys on the Side* (1995)
   (c) Christine Baranski in *The Birdcage* (1996)

166. "Have a wank? It would be easier to raise the Titanic!"
   (a) Hugh Grant in *Maurice* (1987)
   (b) Alfred Molina in *Prick Up Your Ears* (1987)
   (c) Rupert Everett in *Another Country* (1984)

167. "I really want to kiss you, man."
   (a) River Phoenix to Keanu Reeves in *My Own Private Idaho* (1991)
   (b) Matthew Broderick to Harvey Fierstein in *Torch Song Trilogy* (1988)
   (c) Anthony Michael Hall to Will Smith in *Six Degrees of Separation* (1993)

168. "I realize you want to get married, but how many lives do you have to ruin to do it?"
   (a) Rupert Everett to Julia Roberts in *My Best Friend's Wedding* (1997)

(b) Joan Cusack to Kevin Kline in *In & Out* (1997)

(c) Gene Hackman to Dan Futterman in *The Birdcage* (1996)

169. "Next to sex, dishing with the girls is the best thing I know."

(a) James Coco in *Murder By Death* (1974)

(b) James Coco in *The Wild Party* (1975)

(c) James Coco in *Only When I Laugh* (1981)

170. "You know how much the queens love me!"

(a) Bette Midler in *The Rose* (1979)

(b) Shirley MacLaine in *Postcards from the Edge* (1990)

(c) Dorothy Tutin in *Alive & Kicking* (1997)

171. "Does anybody here know how many times I've had to watch *Funny Lady*?"

(a) Joan Cusack in *In & Out* (1997)

(b) Margaret Cho in *It's My Party* (1996)

(c) Marsha Mason in *Only When I Laugh* (1981)

172. "I am not your ordinary, run-of-the-mill transvestite."

(a) Julie Andrews in *Victor/Victoria* (1982)

(b) Jaye Davidson in *The Crying Game* (1992)

(c) Peter Sellers in *Revenge of the Pink Panther* (1978)

173. "I played the bride, now I get to play the groom."

(a) Perry King in *A Different Story* (1978)

(b) Winston Chao in *The Wedding Banquet* (1993)

(c) Uma Thurman in *Henry & June* (1990)

174. "I'm the rock, he's the flake—so that's life."

(a) Richard Jenkins in *Flirting With Disaster* (1996)

(b) Michael T. Weiss in *Jeffrey* (1995)

(c) B.D. Wong in *Father of the Bride* (1991)

175. "Two guys can't love each other."
   (a) Keanu Reeves to River Phoenix in *My Own Private Idaho* (1991)
   (b) Robby Benson to Glynnis O'Connor in *Ode to Billy Joe* (1976)
   (c) Tom Cruise to Brad Pitt in *Interview With the Vampire* (1994)

176. "Never underestimate the power of a woman that's been deprived of the honey pot!"
   (a) Queen Latifah in *Set It Off* (1996)
   (b) Meg Foster in *A Different Story* (1978)
   (c) T. Wendy McMill in *Go Fish* (1994)

177. "Your dick knows what it likes."
   (a) Christopher Guest to Jeff Goldblum in *Beyond Therapy* (1987)
   (b) Adam Nathan to Steve Buscemi in *Parting Glances* (1986)
   (c) Stephen Baldwin to Josh Charles in *Threesome* (1994)

178. "Did you ever wish you were a lesbian? Don't you think it would be *so* much easier?"
   (a) Janeane Garofalo to Winona Ryder in *Reality Bites* (1994)
   (b) Jason Lee to Ben Affleck in *Chasing Amy* (1997)
   (c) Madonna to Rosie O'Donnell in *A League of Their Own* (1992)

179. "I feel like I understand women more—you know, they're more inclusive, they're more open. With men, there's

always a sort of feeling that everything's a competition, and they're so guarded, defensive."

   (a) Mary-Louise Parker in *Boys on the Side* (1995)

   (b) Whoopi Goldberg in *The Associate* (1996)

   (c) Josh Charles in *Threesome* (1994)

180. "What do I look like, a midnight cowboy?"

   (a) Kevin Bacon in *JFK* (1991)

   (b) Will Smith in *Six Degrees of Separation* (1993)

   (c) Robert Beltran in *Scenes from the Class Struggle in Beverly Hills* (1989)

181. "I hope you don't mind me saying so, but I think that I prefer you in *men's* clothing."

   (a) James Garner to Julie Andrews in *Victor/Victoria* (1982)

   (b) Matthew Broderick to Harvey Fierstein in *Torch Song Trilogy* (1988)

   (c) Beryl Reid to Susannah York in *The Killing of Sister George* (1968)

182. "If you don't get sex pretty soon, what will happen is your dick will just get smaller, and smaller, and smaller, till eventually it will just shrivel up, go inside your body, then what do you have? A vagina!"

   (a) Patrick Stewart to Steven Weber in *Jeffrey* (1995)

   (b) Stephen Baldwin to Josh Charles in *Threesome* (1994)

   (c) Bash Hollow to Wally White in *Lie Down With Dogs* (1995)

183. "You've done it with girls?! You never told me that! . . . Did you like it? . . . Could you get it up?"

   (a) River Phoenix to Keanu Reeves in *My Own Private Idaho* (1991)

(b) Jack Thompson to Russell Crowe in *The Sum of Us* (1994)

(c) Woody Allen to Meryl Streep in *Manhattan* (1979)

184. "Boys? Well, there was this one boy that I dated for about three months. Well, we didn't really date, we just held hands and talked about *My Three Sons* a lot, 'cause that was our favorite show."

(a) Paul McCrane in *Fame* (1980)

(b) Nicole Parker in *The Incredibly True Adventures of Two Girls In Love* (1995)

(c) Guinevere Turner in *Go Fish* (1994)

185. "You know what your problem is? You're secretly attracted to women and you're afraid to admit it! You're a closet heterosexual!"

(a) May Chin to Winston Chao in *The Wedding Banquet* (1993)

(b) Laura Flynn Boyle to Josh Charles in *Threesome* (1994)

(c) Christine Baranski to Robin Williams in *The Birdcage* (1996)

186. "I've gone through the motions sleeping with girls exactly three times."

(a) Michael York in *Cabaret* (1972)

(b) Russell Crowe in *The Sum of Us* (1994)

(c) Kristen Scott Thomas in *Four Weddings and a Funeral* (1994)

187. "There *are* easier things in this life than being a drag queen, but I ain't got no choice. You see, try as I may, I just can't walk in flats."

(a) Nathan Lane in *The Birdcage* (1996)

(b) Wesley Snipes in *To Wong Foo . . .* (1995)

(c) Harvey Fierstein in *Torch Song Trilogy* (1988)

188. "These days, gentlemen are an endangered species—unlike bloody drag queens. *We* just keep breeding like rabbits."
   (a) John Cleese in *Privates on Parade* (1984)
   (b) Terence Stamp in *The Adventures of Priscilla, Queen of the Desert* (1994)
   (c) Craig Russell in *Outrageous!* (1977)

189. "I don't know what it is, but there's something that goes on between women. . . . I'm not saying one sex is better than the other, I'm just saying *like* speaks to *like*. Love or whatever doesn't always keep, so you find out what does—if you're lucky."
   (a) Helen Shaver in *Desert Hearts* (1985)
   (b) Jessica Tandy in *Fried Green Tomatoes* (1991)
   (c) Mary-Louise Parker in *Boys on the Side* (1995)

190. "That's what's so great! There's just so many nice lesbians! Just everywhere you look there's lesbians!"
   (a) Chastity Bono in *Bar Girls* (1994)
   (b) Diane Keaton in *The First Wives Club* (1996)
   (c) Jason Lee in *Chasing Amy* (1997)

191. "Let's face it, sweetheart, without Jews, fags, and gypsies, there is no theatre."
   (a) Dustin Hoffman in *Tootsie* (1982)
   (b) Robert Preston in *Victor/Victoria* (1982)
   (c) Mel Brooks in *To Be Or Not to Be* (1983)

192. "Straight sex is better than gay sex—it's written in the Bible."
   (a) Sigourny Weaver in *Jeffrey* (1995)
   (b) Robby Benson in *Ode to Billy Joe* (1976)
   (c) Stephen Baldwin in *Threesome* (1994)

193. "If this is a crush I don't think I can fucking take it if the real thing ever happened."
    (a) Laurel Holloman in *The Incredibly True Adventures of Two Girls in Love* (1995)
    (b) Nancy Allison Wolfe in *Bar Girls* (1994)
    (c) Ben Affleck in *Chasing Amy* (1997)

194. "If you can't commit to our marriage now, what are you going to do when we have a baby?"
    (a) Joan Cusack to Kevin Kline in *In & Out* (1997)
    (b) May Chin to Winston Chao in *The Wedding Banquet* (1993)
    (c) Richard Jenkins to Josh Brolin in *Flirting With Disaster* (1996)

195. "Being a man one day and a woman the next is not an easy thing to do."
    (a) John Lithgow in *The World According to Garp* (1982)
    (b) Terence Stamp in *The Adventures of Priscilla, Queen of the Desert* (1994)
    (c) Julie Andrews in *Victor/Victoria* (1982)

196. "My tits! Where are my tits?"
    (a) Rex Reed in *Myra Breckinridge* (1970)
    (b) Julie Andrews in *Victor/Victoria* (1982)
    (c) Mariel Hemingway in *Personal Best* (1982)

197. "What does *any* man know about the feelings of a woman?"
    (a) Mary-Louise Parker in *Fried Green Tomatoes* (1991)
    (b) Mary-Louise Parker in *Boys on the Side* (1995)
    (c) Barbara Stanwyck in *Walk on the Wild Side* (1962)

198. "I've always wanted to pee standing up."
   (a) Mariel Hemingway in *Personal Best* (1982)
   (b) Raquel Welch in *Myra Breckinridge* (1970)
   (c) Whoopi Goldberg in *The Associate* (1996)

199. "You're not too bright. I like that in a man."
   (a) Bronson Pinchot in *Beverly Hills Cop* (1984)
   (b) Bronson Pinchot in *Beverly Hills Cop III* (1994)
   (c) Bronson Pinchot in *It's My Party* (1996)

200. "Goddamn him. It was going so well. Why did he have to tell me he loved me?"
   (a) Joey Lauren Adams in *Chasing Amy* (1997)
   (b) Harry Hamlin in *Making Love* (1982)
   (c) Steve Weber in *Jeffrey* (1995)

201. "In your heart of hearts you still believe some people are better than others because of the way they make love."
   (a) Rupert Everett in *Another Country* (1984)
   (b) Kenneth Nelson in *Boys in the Band* (1970)
   (c) Harvey Fierstein in *Torch Song Trilogy* (1988)

202. "Dennis Rodman is gay?!"
   (a) Andre Braucher in *Get on the Bus* (1996)
   (b) Whoopi Goldberg in *Eddie* (1996)
   (c) Madonna in *Truth or Dare* (1991)

203. "Straight! He's about as straight as the Yellow Brick Road."
   (a) James Garner in *My Fellow Americans* (1996)
   (b) Alexis Arquette in *Last Exit to Brooklyn* (1989)
   (c) Laurence Luckinbill in *Boys in the Band* (1970)

204. "Sisters?! You don't know what it means to be a sister!"
  - (a) Karen Trumbo to Trisha Wood in *Claire of the Moon* (1992)
  - (b) Patricia Charbonneau to Audra Lindley in *Desert Hearts* (1985)
  - (c) Swoosie Kurtz to Mary Kay Place in *Citizen Ruth* (1996)

205. "You can start by putting the 'do not disturb' sign on the door."
  - (a) Patricia Charbonneau to Helen Shaver in *Desert Hearts* (1985)
  - (b) May Chin to Wai Tung in *The Wedding Banquet* (1993)
  - (c) Lara Flynn Boyle to Josh Charles and Stephen Baldwin in *Threesome* (1994)

206. "A toast before we go into battle: True love, in whatever shape or form it may come, that we all in our dotage be proud to say, 'I was adored once.'"
  - (a) Simon Callow in *Four Weddings and a Funeral* (1994)
  - (b) Mitchell Lichtenstein in *The Wedding Banquet* (1993)
  - (c) Michael York in *Cabaret* (1972)

207. "You have to be true to yourself . . . And if other people don't like it, I know it can be a real drag. But I say if it makes you feel better to have a little mystery about yourself—child, then you go, girl!"
  - (a) Wesley Snipes in *To Wong Foo . . .* (1995)
  - (b) Whoopi Goldberg in *The Associate* (1996)
  - (c) RuPaul in *A Very Brady Sequel* (1996)

4

A Kiss Is Just a Kiss

Below is a list of film actresses, as well as a list of their co-stars. Match the actress in Column A who shared an onscreen kiss with the actress in Column B.

A

208. Drew Barrymore & _____

209. Amanda Donohue & _____

210. Sandra Dumas & _____

211. Greta Garbo & _____

212. Mariel Hemingway & _____

213. Queen Latifah & _____

B

(a) Bibi Anderson

(b) Sammi Davis

(c) Maria de Medeiros

(d) Catherine Deneuve

(e) Patrice Donnelly

(f) Sara Gilbert

214. Susan Sarandon & _____   (g) Lee Grant

215. Kyra Sedgwick & _____   (h) Helen Mirren

216. Uma Thurman & _____   (i) Samantha MacLachlan

217. Shelley Winters & _____   (j) Elizabeth Young

Susan Sarandon

Now, name the film in which the actresses kissed. (No multiple-choice answers this time. You're on your own!)

218. Drew Barrymore and (?) in _____.

219. Amanda Donohue and (?) in _____.

220. Sandra Dumas and (?) in _____.

221. Greta Garbo and (?) in _____.

222. Mariel Hemingway and (?) in _____.

223. Queen Latifah and (?) in _____.

224. Susan Sarandon and (?) in _____.

225. Kyra Sedgwick and (?) in _____.

226. Uma Thurman and (?) in _____.

227. Shelley Winters and (?) in _____.

Below is a list of film actors, as well as a list of their co-stars. Match the actor in column A who shared an onscreen kiss with the actor in column B.

A   **B**

228. Antonio Banderas & _____   (a) Michael Caine

229. Matthew Broderick & _____   (b) Divine

230. Stephen Caffrey & _____   (c) John Dossett

231. Patrick Cassidy & _____   (d) Murray Head

232. Anthony Corlan & _____   (e) Brian Kerwin

233. Peter Finch & _____   (f) John Lone

Christopher Reeve

234. Hugh Grant & _____   (g) Eusebio Poncella

235. Tab Hunter & _____   (h) Campbell Scott

236. Jeremy Irons & _____   (i) Tom Selleck

237. Kevin Kline & _____   (j) James Wilby

238. Christopher Reeve & _____ (k) Michael York

Now, name the film in which the actors kissed. (Again, no multiple-choice answers.)

239. Antonio Banderas and (?) in _____.

240. Matthew Broderick and (?) in _____.

241. Stephen Caffrey and (?) in _____.

242. Patrick Cassidy and (?) in _____.

243. Anthony Corlan and (?) in _____.

244. Peter Finch and (?) in _____.

245. Hugh Grant and (?) in _____.

246. Tab Hunter and (?) in _____.

247. Jeremy Irons and (?) in _____.

248. Kevin Kline and (?) in _____.

249. Christopher Reeve and (?) in _____.

Bar Hopping, Hollywood Style

Below is a list of gay, lesbian, and drag-show bars (Column A), followed by a list of feature films (Column B). Match each of the gay, lesbian, or drag-show bars with the film in which the bar appears.

Column A

250. _____ The Blue Jay

251. _____ The Blue Oyster

252. _____ The Cherry

253. _____ The Frolic Room

254. _____ The Gay Caballero

255. _____ Girl Bar

256. _____ Meow Mix

257. _____ Stud Bar

258. _____ The Tool Box

259. _____ The Watering Hole

Column B

   (a) *Chasing Amy* (1997)
   (b) *The Associate* (1996)
   (c) *Bound* (1996)
   (d) *Bar Girls* (1994)
   (e) *Wayne's World 2* (1993)
   (f) *Torch Song Trilogy* (1988)
   (g) *Police Academy* (1984)
   (h) *The Laughing Policeman* (1974)
   (i) *Some of My Best Friends Are . . .* (1971)
   (j) *P.J.* (1968)

Ellen's "Yep, I'm Gay" Episode

The landmark episode of *Ellen,* in which Ellen Morgan came out as a lesbian, aired April 30, 1997, on ABC. Special guests joined Ellen DeGeneres and the cast for the one-hour program which included therapy sessions, a visit to a lesbian coffeehouse, and an outrageous dream sequence in a supermarket featuring megastars in cameo appearances.

Below is a list of quotes from the coming-out episode of **Ellen** *(Column A), followed by a list of the cast (Column B). Match the actor/actress with the quote that he/she delivered.*

Column A

260. _____ "It's very fashionable to be lesbian now."

261. _____ "I've wasted so much time dating models and actresses, I probably should have just been dating someone like you."

Ellen DeGeneres and Laura Dern

262. _____ "It's funny 'cause the other day I was saying that I don't have enough lesbian friends."

263. _____ "We're running a special this week for lesbians . . . you might want to stock up."

264. _____ "You never see a cake that says, 'Good for you, you're gay!' Maybe Baskin-Robbins in West Hollywood . . ."

265. _____ "I have just one question: Are you gay?"

266. _____ "That'll be a lesbian twenty-nine. . . . $11.29."

267. _____ "If you want to bring a woman home, I'm cool with that—*very* cool."

268. _____ "Would you like to try one of our new granola bars? They're the perfect snack, whether you're on-the-go or in the closet."

269. _____ "What should we call you, gay or lesbian?"

270. _____ "So it's easier to tell your friends what they want to hear?"

271. _____ "Believe me, telling people is always hard."

272. _____ "Do you need some help loading that in your gay car?"

273. _____ "It's so weird, we are so alike."

274. _____ "Everybody sing it, loud and proud!"

Column B

   (a) Ellen DeGeneres (Ellen Morgan)
   (b) Joely Fisher (Paige)
   (c) Jeremy Piven (Spence)
   (d) Clea Lewis (Audrey) *
   (e) David Anthony Higgins (Joe)
   (f) Patrick Bristow (Peter)
   (g) Laura Dern (Susan)

(h) Steven Eckholdt (Richard)
(i) k.d. lang (Janine)
(j) Oprah Winfrey (Therapist)
(k) Billy Bob Thornton
(l) Demi Moore
(m) Gina Gershon
(n) Dwight Yoakam
(o) Melissa Etheridge

7

TV Laugh Tracks

Circle the correct answer.

275. In a 1996 episode of *Roseanne*, Roseanne's mother, Bev (Estelle Parsons), said she read a statistic: "Seventy-three percent of all children raised by homosexuals turn into _____."
   (a) choreographers
   (b) priests
   (c) Democrats
   (d) Diana Ross fans

276. Also on *Roseanne*, when Bev came out as a lesbian, she revealed, "By the end of my marriage, the only way I could have sex with my husband was if I stopped off at the store and _____ first."
   (a) bought myself oysters
   (b) bought myself a *Playboy*
   (c) bought myself a flannel shirt
   (d) rented a Marlene Dietrich movie

Estelle Parsons

277. The 1970's sitcom *Soap* featured a gay character, Jody (played by Billy Crystal), who was referred to in the early episodes as . . .

   (a) the pansy

   (b) the fruit

   (c) the fairy

   (d) Mary

Billy Crystal

278. Also on *Soap,* Jody dated . . .
   (a) a tennis player
   (b) a baseball player
   (c) a football player
   (d) an Olympic diver

279. In a 1993 episode of *Seinfeld,* a published report stated that Jerry was gay. Where did the false report appear?
   (a) a gay magazine
   (b) a college newspaper
   (c) a college alumni newsletter
   (d) a show-biz trade paper

280. In a 1997 episode of *Spin City,* Carter (Michael Boatman) received a visit from an old flame, played by . . .
   (a) Jason Priestly
   (b) Luke Perry

   (c) David Schwimmer

   (d) Matt LeBlanc

281. Who played an effeminate hairdresser in a 1982 episode of *Taxi*?

   (a) Harvey Fierstein

   (b) Dom DeLuise

   (c) Jose Eber

   (d) Ted Danson

282. In the 1996 lesbian wedding episode of *Friends,* Candace Gingrich, Newt Gingrich's half sister, portrayed . . .

   (a) the officiant

   (b) the vegetarian caterer

   (c) the ex-girlfriend of the bride

   (d) the ex-girlfriend of *both* of the brides

283. In a 1992 episode of *Murphy Brown,* which character had a homoerotic dream?

   (a) Corky

   (b) Jim

   (c) Frank

   (d) Miles

284. In a 1978 episode of *WKRP in Cincinnati,* what did the station's news director do after he was barred from locker-room interviews because a player thought he was gay?

   (a) he wrote his Congressman

   (b) he delivered an on-air editorial

   (c) he organized a boycott of the team

   (d) he climbed out on a window ledge

285. On *Ellen,* who was a guest at the dinner party where Peter (Patrick Bristow) met Barrett (Jack Plotnick)?
- (a) Martha Stewart
- (b) Mary Tyler Moore
- (c) Melissa Etheridge
- (d) Emma Thompson

286. In a 1996 issue, *The Advocate* magazine noted that Tim Maculan's portrayal of a waiter "may well be the bitchiest—if not prissiest—gay character on TV ..." On what show does the recurring character appear?
- (a) *Frasier*
- (b) *Cybill*
- (c) *Mad About You*
- (d) *The Frugal Gourmet*

287. On what TV show is food critic Gil Chesterton (played by Edward Hibbert) a recurring character?
- (a) *Frasier*
- (b) *Cybill*
- (c) *Mad About You*
- (d) *The Frugal Gourmet*

288. In a 1996 episode of *3rd Rock from the Sun,* Sally (Kristen Johnston) dropped into a gay bar and was mistaken for ...
- (a) a drag queen
- (b) a gay man
- (c) a lesbian
- (d) Xena: Warrior Princess

289. In a 1997 episode of *Suddenly Susan,* Susan (Brooke Shield) dropped into a gay bar and was mistaken for ...
- (a) a drag queen
- (b) a gay man

    (c) a lesbian

    (d) Xena: Warrior Princess

290. In a 1997 episode of *Wings,* Helen (Crystal Bernard) and Brian (Steven Weber) unknowingly wandered into a drag bar where a drag contest was being presented, hosted by Bella de Ball (played by comic-actor Mark Davis). Pretending to be a drag queen, Helen entered the contest—using the drag name Helena Handbasket—and lip-synched . . .

    (a) "We Are Family"

    (b) "I Will Survive"

    (c) "Mama Mia"

    (d) "New York, New York"

291. The winner of the drag contest in that episode of *Wings* was awarded . . .

    (a) $100

    (b) $200

    (c) $250

    (d) a make-over

292. Who did *not* appear in the episode of *Roseanne* in which Leon and Scott (Martin Mull and Fred Willard) celebrated their commitment ceremony?

    (a) Milton Berle

    (b) Mariel Hemingway

    (c) bare-chested muscle men

    (d) religious-right protestors

293. Who played the officiant in the gay wedding episode of *Roseanne?*

    (a) Norm MacDonald

    (b) Norm Crosby

(c) Rodney Dangerfield

(d) Andrew Dice Clay

294. In the episode of *Roseanne* in which Mariel Hemingway and Roseanne kissed, Lois Bromfield (comic and *Roseanne* scriptwriter) played a bar patron who tried to pick up . . .

(a) Roseanne

(b) Jackie (Laurie Metcalf)

(c) Nancy (Sandra Bernhard)

(d) Leon (Fred Willard)

295. On *Mad About You,* when Paul Buchman's sister, Debbie (Robin Bartlett), came out to her family, her mother . . .

(a) phoned P-FLAG (Parents & Friends of Lesbians and Gays)

(b) phoned her therapist

(c) almost fainted

(d) almost jumped out a window

296. On *The Simpsons,* according to a police record, the character Waylon Smithers has a rub-on ankle tattoo depicting what gay icon?

(a) Barbra Streisand

(b) Judy Garland

(c) Liza Minnelli

(d) Michelangelo's David

297. Who provides the voice for Waylon Smithers on *The Simpsons?*

(a) Al Franken

(b) Harry Shearer

(c) Martin Mull

(d) Conan O'Brian

298. In a 1997 episode of *The Simpsons* titled "Homer's Homophobia," who provided the voice for an antiques dealer?

(a) Harvey Fierstein
(b) John Waters
(c) John Ritter
(d) Fred Willard

299. In a 1975 episode of *Barney Miller,* police detective "Wojo" Wojohowicz booked . . .

(a) a lesbian Peeping Tom
(b) a gay purse snatcher
(c) a cross-dressing shoplifter
(d) a bisexual jaywalker

300. In the 1994 Thanksgiving episode of *Grace Under Fire,* Grace received a visit from a gay in-law (played by stand-up comic Barry Steiger). The character was Grace's ex-husband's . . .

(a) brother
(b) cousin
(c) nephew
(d) Army buddy

301. In a 1991 episode of Fox's *Roc,* who played Roc's uncle, who revealed that he was gay and in love with a white man?

(a) James Earl Jones
(b) Billy Dee Williams
(c) Louis Gossett, Jr.
(d) Richard Roundtree

302. Alan Sues frequently appeared on the 1960's series

Rowan & Martin's Laugh-In as an effeminate character named Big Al. What was Big Al's occupation?

    (a) porno star

    (b) movie critic

    (c) sports commentator

    (d) construction worker

303. In a 1980 episode of *Taxi*, a bisexual man dated Elaine (Marilu Henner) but also wanted to date . . .

    (a) Alex (Judd Hirsch)

    (b) Tony (Tony Danza)

    (c) Bobby (Jeff Conaway)

    (d) Louie (Danny Devito)

304. The lead character of the 1981 made-for-TV movie *Sidney Shorr: A Girl's Best Friend* was gay. It was later turned into a series, but with no mention of the character's homosexuality. Who was the star of *Sidney Shorr*?

    (a) Dom DeLuise

    (b) Charles Nelson Reilly

    (c) Tony Randall

    (d) Jack Klugman

305. In a 1992 episode of *Cheers*, who guest-starred as an old high school boyfriend of Rebecca's (Kirstie Alley) who revealed that he was gay?

    (a) Judd Hirsch

    (b) Parker Stevenson

    (c) John Travolta

    (d) Harvey Fierstein

306. In a 1986 episode of *The Golden Girls*, which one of the

characters received a visit from an old friend who was a lesbian?

(a) Dorothy (Bea Arthur)
(b) Rose (Betty White)
(c) Blanche (Rue McClanahan)
(d) Sophia (Estelle Getty)

307. On HBO's *Tracey Takes On . . .* , Julie Kavner played a lesbian professional golfer named . . .

(a) Barbie
(b) Buffy
(c) Muffy
(d) Midge

308. Also on *Tracey Takes On . . .* , Tracey Ullman played a gay male flight attendant named . . .

(a) Torey
(b) Trevor
(c) Truman
(d) Truffle

309. On *Daddy's Girls,* the short-lived sitcom in 1994, who played the gay sidekick to Dudley Moore?

(a) Jim J. Bullock
(b) Richard Simmons
(c) Harvey Fierstein
(d) Peter Cook

310. In a 1997 episode of *Married . . . With Children,* Amanda Bearse played dual roles, Marcy and her lesbian . . .

(a) sister
(b) cousin
(c) aunt
(d) mother

Amanda Bearse

311. What ABC affiliate refused to air the coming-out episode of *Ellen?*
- (a) Birmingham, Alabama
- (b) St. Louis, Missouri
- (c) Nashville, Tennessee
- (d) Austin, Texas

TV Drama Queens

Circle the correct answer.

312. What performer, also known as a TV game-show personality, played a bisexual cop in a 1977 episode of *Starsky & Hutch*?
 (a) Orson Bean *(To Tell the Truth)*
 (b) Art Fleming (original *Jeopardy)*
 (c) Paul Lynde (original *Hollywood Squares)*
 (d) Kitty Carlisle *(To Tell the Truth)*

313. In the same episode of *Starsky & Hutch,* who played a female impersonator?
 (a) Charles Pierce
 (b) Milton Berle
 (c) John Davidson
 (d) Kitty Carlisle

314. Tina Louise, best known for playing Ginger on *Gilligan's*

Island, appeared in the 1975 telefilm *The Homicide of Jenny Storm.* What role did she portray?
- (a) a bisexual paralegal
- (b) a lesbian dental assistant
- (c) a transsexual receptionist
- (d) a closeted movie star

315. In a 1991 episode of *L.A. Law,* Amanda Donohue and Michele Greene presented what GLAAD (Gay and Lesbian Alliance Against Defamation) called "the ＿＿＿＿＿＿ lesbian kiss on a network series."
- (a) sexiest
- (b) longest
- (c) most convincing
- (d) first

Amanda Donohue

316. In an episode of the 1970's series *Marcus Welby, M.D.*, Dr. Welby (played by Robert Young) advised a patient who was upset over his homosexual tendencies to . . .
    (a) see a psychiatrist
    (b) see *Boys in the Band*
    (c) take a vacation in San Francisco
    (d) get a second opinion

317. In another episode of *Marcus Welby, M.D.*, a boy was raped by a junior high teacher. The boy named the attacker only after his family told him that he was "_____."
    (a) still a man
    (b) still loved
    (c) still heterosexual
    (d) still in the will

318. In 1989, *thirtysomething* aired a scene between two gay men . . .
    (a) in a gay bar after a riot
    (b) at a family reunion after coming out to the folks
    (c) at the mall after a clearance sale
    (d) in bed after sex

319. In a 1991 episode of *Northern Exposure*, the town of Cicely, Alaska, was in turmoil about selling a house to a gay male couple who wanted to convert it to . . .
    (a) a bed-and-breakfast
    (b) a gay bar
    (c) a karaoke bar
    (d) a sushi bar

320. In the 1988 made-for-TV film titled *Liberace*, who played Liberace's mother?
    (a) Betty White

(b) Rue McClanahan
(c) Bea Arthur
(d) Estelle Getty

321. Who was the first actor to play Steven Carrington, a bisexual character on *Dynasty*?
    (a) Jack Coleman
    (b) Al Corley

322. A 1972 episode of *The New Doctors* featured a love triangle involving a male intern, a lesbian, and a nurse who couldn't choose between them. Who played the nurse?
    (a) Donna Reed
    (b) Donna Mills
    (c) Hayley Mills
    (d) John Mills

323. A number of affiliates refused to air a 1993 *CBS Schoolbreak Special* about a teenager who was ostracized because . . .
    (a) he had two lesbian mothers
    (b) he befriended the class sissy
    (c) he asked a boy to the prom
    (d) he ran like a girl

324. On *All My Children*, Chris Bruno played Michael Delaney, a gay character who was a high school . . .
    (a) history teacher
    (b) drama teacher
    (c) football coach
    (d) swim coach

325. On what daytime drama did Donna Pescow (who appeared in the film *Saturday Night Fever*) play a lesbian?
    (a) *One Life to Live*

(b) *Days of Our Lives*
(c) *As the World Turns*
(d) *All My Children*

326. On what daytime drama did a straight male character address high school students about AIDS, and confront a student's verbal attack with the following retort? " 'Faggot' is a mean word to apply to someone who understands love."
(a) *The City*
(b) *The Young and the Restless*
(c) *General Hospital*
(d) *Days of Our Lives*

327. In the 1992 made-for-TV film *Doing Time on Maple Drive*, one of the characters was gay. Who played the gay character's older brother?
(a) Dana Carvey
(b) Bill Murray
(c) James Belushi
(d) Jim Carrey

328. What television show was attacked by gay groups because of an episode which portrayed lesbian owners of an old-age home as predatory killers?
(a) *Marcus Welby, M.D.*
(b) *Policewoman*
(c) *Matlock*
(d) *Murder, She Wrote*

329. In a 1985 episode of *Trapper John, M.D.*, a nurse assisted a former boyfriend who was gay and HIV-positive. Who played the nurse?
(a) Liza Minnelli
(b) Lorna Luft

(c) Jim Bailey
(d) Peter Allen

330. In the 1996 made-for-TV film *Two Mothers for Zachary,* Valerie Bertinelli portrayed a lesbian mother who lost custody of her child to her own mother. Who played Bertinelli's mother?
(a) Lynn Redgrave
(b) Vanessa Redgrave
(c) Diane Weiss
(d) Julie Andrews

331. In the 1986 made-for-TV film *My Two Loves,* Mariette Hartley played a widow who became involved with both a man and a woman. Barry Newman played the man. Who played the woman?
(a) Lynn Redgrave
(b) Vanessa Redgrave
(c) Diane Weiss
(d) Julie Andrews

332. In the 1991 made-for-TV film *Our Sons,* Hugh Grant and Zeljko Ivanek portrayed lovers. Ann-Margaret played Ivanek's mother. Who played Grant's mother?
(a) Lynn Redgrave
(b) Vanessa Redgrave
(c) Diane Weiss
(d) Julie Andrews

333. In the 1986 made-for-TV film *Second Serve,* who portrayed transsexual tennis-pro Renee Richards?
(a) Lynn Redgrave
(b) Vanessa Redgrave

(c) Diane Weiss

(d) Julie Andrews

334. The British production *Portrait of a Marriage* dramatized the marriage between lesbian novelist Vita Sackville-West and homosexual diplomat Harold Nicolson. When PBS aired it, according to reports, how many minutes of sex scenes were cut?

(a) 6

(b) 34

(c) 49

(d) 69

Wilson Cruz

335. In 1976, as part of its Bicentennial salute to great Americans, CBS presented a dramatization starring Rip Torn as Walt Whitman. Who played Peter Boyle, Whitman's lover?

(a) Parker Stevenson

(b) Brad Davis

(c) Michael Thomas

(d) Richard Chamberlain

336. Wilson Cruz portrayed TV's first recurring gay teen on *My So-Called Life*. What was his character's name?

(a) Jimmy

(b) Jamie

(c) Eddie

(d) Ricky

337. On *Party of Five*, Mitchell Anderson plays a gay man who teaches . . .

(a) voice

(b) violin

(c) piano

(d) cello

338. When *Armistead Maupin's Tales of the City* debuted on PBS, it was presented as . . .

(a) a five-part series

(b) a six-part series

(c) a seven-part series

(d) an eight-part series

339. On what TV show did Bill Brochtrup play a gay man who worked as a secretary at a police precinct?

(a) *Law & Order*

(b) *N.Y.P.D. Blue*

(c) *Hooperman*

(d) *Policewoman*

340. In a 1997 episode of *E.R.*, Dr. Maggie Doyle (Jorja Fox) came out as a lesbian. Downplaying Maggie's lesbian revelation, coproducer Dr. Neal Baer noted to the *Advocate,* ''We also found out that she's a vegetarian in that episode and that she collects _____.''

    (a) coins

    (b) antiques

    (c) Barbie dolls

    (d) guns

Talking Heads

Circle the correct answer.

341. On *The Rosie O'Donnell Show,* Elton John said if he and Barbra Streisand conceived a child, "With my luck, we'd give birth to _____."
   (a) a music critic
   (b) an informant for *The National Enquirer*
   (c) a twin pair of Grammy Awards
   (d) a ten-pound gay nose

342. On *Live With Regis & Kathie Lee,* Kathie Lee Gifford commented about a guest in the following way. "We all live to get our panty hose off. _____ is no different than any of us."
   (a) RuPaul
   (b) Dennis Rodman

(c) Wesley Snipes

(d) Ellen DeGeneres

343. Who was a guest on a 1991 panel on *The Sally Jessy Raphael Show* examining the topic "Lesbians Who Don't Look Like Lesbians"?

(a) actress Amanda Bearse

(b) Martina Navratilova's ex, Judy Nelson

(c) comic Suzanne Westenhoefer

(d) radio host Howard Stern

344. Appearing on Fox-TV's *The Arsenio Hall Show* in 1993, comic Lea DeLaria proclaimed, "It's the 1990s, it's hip to be queer, and I'm _____."

(a) a big butch

(b) a big femme

(c) a big dyke

(d) a big loudmouth

345. When comic Kate Clinton appeared on *The Arsenio Hall Show,* she declared, "Some people wouldn't know a lesbian if _____."

(a) their mouth was full of one

(b) their butt was kicked by a pair of Birkenstocks

(c) their favorite singer was k.d. lang

(d) their tennis partner was Martina Navratilova

346. On VH-1's *The RuPaul Show,* to what guest did RuPaul say, "Your lips are so big and juicy!"?

(a) Whoopi Goldberg

(b) Cher

(c) Goldie Hawn

(d) Dennis Rodman

Kate Clinton

347. In 1976, a TV interviewer asked Holly Woodlawn (star of Andy Warhol's *Trash*) the following series of questions: "What *are* you? Are you a woman trapped in a man's body? Are you a heterosexual? Are you a homosexual? A transvestite? A transsexual? *What* is the answer to the question?" Who was the TV interviewer?

  (a) Geraldo Rivera
  (b) Hugh Downs
  (c) Merv Griffin
  (d) Barbara Walters

348. What was Holly Woodlawn's response to the interviewer's questioning?
   (a) "A woman trapped in a man's body, darling."
   (b) "A homosexual, darling."
   (c) "A transsexual, darling."
   (d) "But, darling, what difference does it *make* as long as you look fabulous?"

349. On what TV show in 1985 did a spokesperson for a group called the Christian Voice comment on the increased number of gay characters in films in the following way? "There must be homosexuals within the industry who have made the decision to portray [homosexuality] more than ever before, otherwise why would it exist?"
   (a) *20/20*
   (b) *Meet the Press*
   (c) *The Today Show*
   (d) *Donahue*

350. Interviewing Funny Gay Males (Jaffe Cohen, Danny McWilliams, and Bob Smith) on *The Joan Rivers Show,* Rivers asked McWilliams, "What does your mother think of you coming on the show?" The gay comic responded, "My mother is on the rooftops in ＿＿＿＿ cutting the cable wires!"
   (a) Brooklyn
   (b) Manhattan
   (c) Queens
   (d) Staten Island

351. What talk-show host posed the following question to comic Bob Smith? "As a heterosexual man, there are some women that I look at that I'm attracted to, but there are

many, many more that I'm *not* attracted to. Is it the same if you're homosexual, that you're not attracted to every guy?''
(a) Maury Povich
(b) Geraldo Rivera
(c) Larry King
(d) Tom Snyder

352. On what show did stand-up comic Jason Stuart come out?
(a) *Sally Jessy Raphael*
(b) *Geraldo*
(c) *Oprah*
(d) *Martha Stewart Living*

353. On the syndicated talk show *Rolonda,* the host introduced HIV-positive comic Steve Moore as . . .
(a) a genius
(b) a good will ambassador
(c) a laugh riot
(d) death defying

354. Also on *Rolonda,* a young woman in the studio audience asked a famous guest, ''Are you straight?'' The guest responded, ''Yes. Why? Was there an invitation coming?'' Who was the guest?
(a) Queen Latifah
(b) Patti LaBelle
(c) Whoopi Goldberg
(d) Dennis Rodman

355. Who cracked the following joke at the opening of his show? ''More news from the friendly folks at the Heaven's Gate cult. Yesterday, another cult member boarded the

Mother Ship. . . . He said he did not leave with the original group because he didn't want to miss that episode of *Ellen.*"

  (a) Jay Leno
  (b) David Letterman
  (c) Bill Maher
  (d) Conan O'Brien

356. Who delivered the following quip? "Wendy's [is] probably sorry they yanked [their] ads from *Ellen* after seeing the huge ratings. In fact, today Dave Thomas announced, 'Yeah, Wendy's a lesbian. Oh, yeah, all the time.' "

  (a) Jay Leno
  (b) David Letterman
  (c) Bill Maher
  (d) Conan O'Brien

Channel Surfing

Circle the correct answer.

357. Within a two-week period in 1988, which two networks aired a made-for-TV film about Liberace?
   (a) ABC and CBS
   (b) CBS and NBC
   (c) NBC and ABC

358. Mario Lopez (from TV's *Saved By The Bell*) starred in *Breaking the Surface: The Greg Louganis Story,* which aired on . . .
   (a) Fox
   (b) PBS
   (c) USA Network

359. Stand-up comic Suzanne Westenhoefer was nomianted for an Ace Award for her cable special. On what cable channel did it air?

   (a) HBO

   (b) Lifetime

   (c) Comedy Central

Mario Lopez and Greg Louganis

360. What network aired *Serving in Silence: The Margarethe Cammermeyer Story,* the true story of a lesbian who was ousted from the Army National Guard?
   (a) ABC
   (b) CBS
   (c) NBC

361. What network aired *Sgt. Matlovich vs. the U.S. Air Force,* the true story of a gay man who was ousted from the Air Force?
   (a) ABC
   (b) CBS
   (c) NBC

362. The off-Broadway play *Fifth of July* was adapted for television and starred Richard Thomas and Jeff Daniels as lovers. It aired on . . .
   (a) PBS
   (b) HBO
   (c) Showtime

363. *As Is* (based on the stage play) starred Robert Carradine and Jonathan Hadary as ex-lovers, one of whom was diagnosed with AIDS. It aired on . . .
   (a) PBS
   (b) HBO
   (c) Showtime

364. *More Than Friends: The Coming Out of Heidi Leiter,* a made-for-TV film, told the true story of two lesbians who attended their high school prom together. It aired on . . .
   (a) USA Network
   (b) Showtime
   (c) HBO

Suzanne Westenhoefer

365. *Sara,* a short-lived sitcom in 1985, featured Geena Davis as a lawyer and Bronson Pinchot as her gay cohort. On what network did it air?

   (a) ABC

   (b) CBS

   (c) NBC

366. Also in 1985, *An Early Frost* was a made-for-TV film with Aidan Quinn as a gay lawyer who returned home to inform

his parents, played by Gena Rowlands and Ben Gazzara, that he was HIV-positive. On what network did it air?

(a) ABC

(b) CBS

(c) NBC

367. *The Women of Brewster Place,* a miniseries produced by Oprah Winfrey's Harpo Productions and directed by Donna Deitch *(Desert Hearts),* included a lesbian couple. On what network did it air?

(a) ABC

(b) CBS

(c) NBC

368. *Brothers* was the first original sitcom produced for cable. One of the three brothers, played by Paul Regina, was gay. On what cable channel did it air?

(a) Comedy Central

(b) Showtime

(c) HBO

369. What cable channel aired a series of specials featuring gay and lesbian stand-up comics, *Out There* (hosted by Lea DeLaria), *Out There II* (hosted by Amanda Bearse), and *Out There in Hollywood* (hosted by Scott Thompson)?

(a) Comedy Central

(b) Showtime

(c) HBO

Musical Notes

Circle the correct answer.

370. Who released a single titled "Queer to the Core"?
    (a) Bronski Beat
    (b) Pet Shop Boys
    (c) Erasure
    (d) Pansy Division

371. Joking about plans to record an album, *Xena : Warrior Princes s*star Lucy Lawless told *TV Guide* ,"I'm thinking of doing _____'s greatest hits."
    (a) k.d. lang
    (b) Melissa Etheridge
    (c) RuPaul
    (d) Sappho

Indigo Girls

372.

Indigo Girls Amy Ray and Emily Saliers met in their high school . . .
- (a) softball team
- (b) basketball team
- (c) audio-visual club
- (d) choir

373. In a British magazine, Neil Tennant of the Pet Shop Boys stated, "I just thought it would be pathetic to turn _____ and not come out. So I did it."
- (a) 30

(b) 35

(c) 40

(d) 45

374. Who joined the Pet Shop Boys on the 1987 song "What Have I Done to Deserve This"?

(a) Elton John

(b) Bruce Springsteen

(c) Dusty Springfield

(d) Boy George

375. Who recorded a song called "I Kissed A Girl"?

(a) Ani diFranco

(b) Phranc

(c) the Indigo Girls

(d) Jill Sobule

376. Jimmy Somerville formerly performed with . . .

(a) Bronski Beat

(b) Pet Shop Boys

(c) Erasure

(d) Pansy Division

377. Who recorded the title song for the film *The Crying Game?*

(a) Elton John

(b) Bruce Springsteen

(c) Dusty Springfield

(d) Boy George

378. Who sang the title song for *Philadelphia?*

(a) Elton John

(b) Bruce Springsteen
(c) Dusty Springfield
(d) Boy George

379. Which of Queen's singles was rereleased to raise funds for AIDS research?
(a) "Bohemian Rhapsody"
(b) "You're My Best Friend"
(c) "Someone to Love"
(d) "We Are the Champions"

380. The first album produced by Olivia Records, *Meg Christian: I Know You Know,* includes a song titled "Ode to _____."
(a) a Vegetarian
(b) a Gym Teacher
(c) Sensible Shoes
(d) Billie Jean

381. The film *Boys on the Side* includes a performance by . . .
(a) Cris Williamson and Tret Fure
(b) the Indigo Girls
(c) Janis Ian
(d) Phranc

382. The Flirtations, a gay a cappella singing group that appeared in the film *Philadelphia,* sang at a same-sex commitment ceremony which was televised on . . .
(a) *Donahue*
(b) *Ricki Lake*
(c) *Oprah*
(d) *Jenny Jones*

383. What Madonna song is covered on *Sweet Enuf 2 Eat,* the debut album by gay pop group Men Out Loud?

  (a) "Vogue"
  (b) "Express Yourself"
  (c) "Justify My Love"
  (d) "Like a Virgin"

Men Out Loud

Center Stage

Circle the correct answer.

384. In what play did gay Olympic diver Greg Louganis make his New York stage debut as a replacement?
  (a) *Party*
  (b) *Jeffrey*
  (c) *Cats*
  (d) *Grease*

385. Anne Bancroft was cast as Ma in the film version of *Torch Song Trilogy*. Who played the role in the Broadway production?
  (a) Betty White
  (b) Rue McClanahan
  (c) Bea Arthur
  (d) Estelle Getty

386. While hosting the fiftieth anniversary of the Tony

Awards in 1996, who commented, "Fifty years of the marriage of art and bucks. . . . If Clinton had his way, Art won't be allowed to marry Buck"?

(a) Angela Lansbury
(b) Carol Channing
(c) Bea Arthur
(d) Nathan Lane

387. In the play *Sister Mary Ignatius Explains It All For You* by Christopher Durang, the nun says gay men "do that thing that makes Jesus _____."

(a) cry blood
(b) puke
(c) retaliate with natural disasters
(d) create more heterosexuals

388. Who won the Tony award for his portrayal of gay writer Truman Capote in *Tru*?

(a) Anthony Perkins
(b) Roddy McDowall
(c) Robert Morse
(d) Charles Nelson Reilly

389. In the film version of *Tea and Sympathy* (1956), John Kerr played Tom, a sensitive young man who's wrongly suspected of being homosexual. Who played the role on Broadway?

(a) Anthony Perkins
(b) Roddy McDowall
(c) Robert Morse
(d) Charles Nelson Reilly

390. In the musical *Hair,* an army psychiatrist asks Woof if he is homosexual. Woof responds, "I wouldn't throw _____ out of bed, but no, I'm not homosexual."
  (a) David Bowie
  (b) Mick Jagger
  (c) John Lennon
  (d) Paul McCartney

391. *Making Porn,* a play about the gay adult entertainment industry, ran in several cities with various stars before playing in New York. Who starred in the production when it made its off-Broadway debut in 1996 at the Actors' Playhouse in New York?
  (a) Ryan Idol
  (b) Jeff Stryker
  (c) Rex Chandler
  (d) Simon Rex

392. Who wrote and performed in a stage play titled *The Only Thing Worse You Could Have Told Me?*
  (a) Amanda Bearse (from *Married . . . With Children*)
  (b) Michael Boatman (from *Spin City*)
  (c) Dan Butler (from *Frasier*)
  (d) Mitchell Anderson (from *Party of Five*)

393. Who made his stage debut at age 15 by playing Kate in Shakespeare's *The Taming of the Shrew?*
  (a) Sir John Gielgud
  (b) Sir Ian McKellen
  (c) Lord Laurence Olivier
  (d) Rupert Everett

394. Steven J. McCarthy—a.k.a. Madame Dish, host of the cable cooking show *Dish* and star of the stage show *Strip—*

began his career as a child actor. What theatrical role marked his first professional acting job?

   (a) The Artful Dodger in *Oliver*

   (b) Frederic in *The Sound of Music*

   (c) Peter Pan in *Peter Pan*

   (d) Wendy in *Peter Pan*

395. Comic-actor Mark Davis—who plays Ashley, a gay recurring character on TV's *Fired Up*—wrote and performed in a stage play titled "Faggot With _____."

   (a) an Agenda

   (b) an Attitude

   (c) a Gun

   (d) Heterosexual Tendencies

Madame Dish (a.k.a. Steven J. McCarthy and Her Naughty Boys

396. Jason Alexander was cast as Buzz in the film version of *Love! Valour! Compassion!* Who played the role on Broadway?

  (a) Nathan Lane
  (b) Joel Grey
  (c) Tony Roberts
  (d) Julie Andrews

397. Playwright Terrence McNally *(Love! Valour! Compassion!)* opined, "The greatest gay character ever written is _____."

  (a) Buzz in *Love! Valour! Compassion!*
  (b) Donald in *Boys in the Band*
  (c) Jeffrey in *Jeffrey*
  (d) Hamlet in *Hamlet*

People . . .

Circle the correct answer.

398. What couple published a statement in response to speculation they are gay?
   (a) John Travolta and Kelly Preston
   (b) Tom Cruise and Nicole Kidman
   (c) Richard Gere and Cindy Crawford
   (d) Siegfried and Roy

399. Who made his American made-for-TV debut by playing a gay man who picks up and gropes a hitchhiker?
   (a) Arnold Schwarzenegger
   (b) Jean Claude Van Damme
   (c) Antonio Banderas
   (d) Hugh Grant

400. Who turned down a gay role in the film version of *A Chorus Line* (1985) because, according to a statement in *Jet* magazine, "People already think I'm that way—homo—because of my voice, which I'm not."
- (a) Johnny Mathis
- (b) Michael Jackson
- (c) Little Richard
- (d) Eddie Murphy

401. Comic Lea DeLaria told *People* magazine that her act was an attempt to impress . . .
- (a) her mother
- (b) her father
- (c) her therapist
- (d) Sigourney Weaver

Lea DeLaria

402. What does singer Janis Ian call her partner?
(a) Miss Lesbian
(b) Ms. Lesbian
(c) Mrs. Lesbian
(d) Mr. Lesbian

403. Gay porn star Steven Marks was formerly . . .
(a) a TV weatherman in Chicago
(b) a circus clown in Russia
(c) a cable-TV talk-show host in New York
(d) a chorus boy in Las Vegas

404. Film director Julie Cypher *(Teresa's Tattoo)* is Melissa Etheridge's partner, and ex-wife of . . .
(a) John Phillips
(b) Lou Diamond Phillips
(c) Phil Donahue
(d) Martina Navratilova

405. At what event did Melissa Etheridge come out publicly?
(a) the 1993 March on Washington
(b) the 1993 Triangle Ball in Washington, D.C.
(c) the 1994 Gay Games in New York City
(d) at half-time of the 1994 Super Bowl

406. Accepting his Academy Award for his portrayal of a gay man in *Philadelphia,* Tom Hanks thanked two people—"two of the finest gay Americans that I had the good fortune to be associated with." They were his classmate and his high school . . .
(a) history teacher
(b) drama teacher
(c) football coach
(d) cafeteria lady

407. Who publicly expressed a fear of going to jail because of the lesbians?
   (a) Sophia Loren
   (b) Heidi Fleiss
   (c) Zsa Zsa Gabor
   (d) Jim Baker

408. In a 1996 *Advocate* readers' poll, whose performance was named "favorite portrayal of a lesbian in a feature film"?
   (a) Cher in *Silkwood*
   (b) Whoopi Goldberg in *Boys on the Side*
   (c) Patricia Charbonneau in *Desert Hearts*
   (d) Rosie O'Donnell in *A League of Their Own*

409. In the same poll, whose film performance was picked as "the most offensive portrayal of a lesbian"?
   (a) Lotte Lenya in *From Russia With Love*
   (b) Barbara Stanwyck in *Walk on the Wild Side*
   (c) Shirley MacLaine in *The Children's Hour*
   (d) the entire cast of *Claire of the Moon*

410. Nick Scotti, who plays Frankie Zito in *Kiss Me, Guido,* was born in . . .
   (a) Queens
   (b) Brooklyn
   (c) the Bronx
   (d) Staten Island

411. Who described *Glen or Glenda* in the following way? "Sensational but sincere 'docu-fantasy' about transvestism, could well be the worst movie ever made."
   (a) Rex Reed
   (b) Liz Smith

(c) Leonard Maltin

(d) J. Edgar Hoover

412. Explaining why she accepted a role in the CBS mini-series *Mario Puzo's The Last Don,* k.d. lang told a reporter, "I took the role of Dita because she's exactly like me—a demanding feminist _____."

(a) lesbian

(b) dyke

(c) bitch

(d) vegetarian

413. Who called comic Kate Clinton "the kind of lesbian you can take home to your parents"?

(a) *Parents* magazine

(b) *The Village Voice*

(c) *The Los Angeles Times*

(d) Urvashi Vaid

414. Entertainment mogul David Geffen, who is gay, told *Entertainment Weekly,* "There is not an entertainment company, not one, that doesn't have gay people working there. Some are in the closet, but it isn't always for fear of their jobs. They just _____, and they pay a price for that choice."

(a) live with someone of the opposite sex

(b) live in conservative Orange County

(c) live in gay-friendly West Hollywood

(d) live in shame and embarrassment

415. Terry Sweeny, the gay comedic actor/writer who appeared with the 1986–87 cast of *Saturday Night Live,* said

in a *People* magazine interview, "A house, a husband, and _____, I have everything I ever wanted."

(a) a dog

(b) a BMW

(c) a houseboy

(d) a prenuptial agreement

416. According to an *Us* magazine profile on Rupert Everett, who did the actor call the "ultimate fag hag"?

(a) Elizabeth Taylor

(b) Barbra Streisand

(c) Madonna

(d) Julia Roberts

417. Responding to a 1995 Gallup poll, what percentage of Americans said they wouldn't have a problem watching a gay actor in a straight love scene?

(a) 32%

(b) 42%

(c) 52%

(d) 62%

418. Who expressed the following sentiment about the character Kristy McNichol played on the 1970's TV series *Family*? "I loved Buddy, the first little tomboy on TV."

(a) Jodie Foster

(b) Rosie O'Donnell

(c) Paula Poundstone

(d) Kristy McNichol

419. On E! Entertainment Television, who delivered the following quip? "If you're homosexual you like men, if you're gay you know all the words to *South Pacific*."

(a) John Henson on *Talk Soup*

(b) Michael Musto on *The Gossip Show*

(c) Dick Dietrick on *Nightstand*

(d) Steve Kmetko on *E! News Daily*

420. When a London *Times* reporter asked Peter Finch how he could possibly kiss a man in *Sunday, Bloody Sunday,* the actor responded, "I just closed my eyes and thought of _____."

(a) my first girlfriend

(b) my paycheck

(c) England

(d) the Queen

421. Who expressed the following opinion about the 1982 film *Personal Best?* "According to this movie, lesbianism is just something you catch in the locker room, like athlete's foot."

(a) Vito Russo

(b) Leonard Maltin

(c) Rex Reed

(d) Billie Jean King

422. In a commentary in an April 1977 issue of *Time* magazine, playwright and screenwriter Paul Rudnick *(In & Out, Addams Family Values* and *Jeffrey)* mused, "How come when a movie like *The Birdcage* makes more than $100 million, it's no longer considered a gay movie, but _____?"

(a) a straight movie

(b) a family movie

(c) a date movie

(d) a hit

423. Keeping a diary during the shoot of *In & Out,* screenwriter Paul Rudnick related in *Premiere* magazine that a scene

from the movie-within-the-movie, which is supposed to take place in a rice paddy in Vietnam, was actually filmed outdoors in . . .

(a) Queens
(b) Brooklyn
(c) the Bronx
(d) Staten Island

424. Who was the first actor to be nominated for an Academy Award for an openly gay role?

(a) Peter Finch
(b) William Hurt
(c) Tom Hanks
(d) Jaye Davidson

Sandra Bernhard, Candace Gingrich, and Melissa Etheridge

425. For what film did Rock Hudson receive an Academy Award nomination?

   (a) *Giant* (1956)

   (b) *A Farewell to Arms* (1957)

   (c) *Magnificent Obsession* (1954)

   (d) *Captain Lightfoot* (1955)

426. Sandra Bernhard made her film debut in . . .

   (a) *Cheech & Chong's Nice Dreams*

   (b) *The King of Comedy*

   (c) *Follow That Bird*

   (d) *Track 29*

427. In the 1956 film *Tea and Sympathy,* Deborah Kerr uttered, ''Years from now when you talk about this—and you will—be kind.'' Who repeated that quote in another film?

   (a) Harry Hamlin to Michael Ontkean in *Making Love* (1982)

   (b) Rupert Everett to James Harcourt in *Another Country* (1984)

   (c) Rupert Everett to Julia Roberts in *My Best Friend's Wedding* (1997)

   (d) Lily Tomlin to John Travola in *Moment by Moment* (1978)

428. In the book *The Unofficial Gay Manual* by Kevin DiLallo and Jack Krumholz, what star is described in the following way? ''We were there for her and she for us at a time when she was a nobody and it wasn't chic to be gay.''

   (a) Barbra Streisand

   (b) Bette Midler

   (c) Bette Davis

   (d) Liberace

429. In a May 1997 article, *People* magazine reported, "By coming out, [Ellen] DeGeneres and [Anne] Heche, who once dated _____, are the first Hollywood stars to engage in an openly gay romance."
   (a) Tommy Lee Jones
   (b) Harrison Ford
   (c) Antonio Banderas
   (d) Steve Martin

430. Who remarked in a *Life* magazine interview that "a homosexual [male] is a female soul in a male's body"?
   (a) Zsa Zsa Gabor
   (b) Marilyn Monroe
   (c) Mae West
   (d) John Wayne

431. Who commented about Tom Cruise to *The Chicago Tribune* in the following way? "This man is so heterosexual. Every time he touched me in the movie we had to do a reshoot because I blushed."
   (a) Bonnie Hunt *(Jerry Maguire)*
   (b) Kelly Preston *(Jerry Maguire)*
   (c) Nicole Kidman *(Far and Away)*
   (d) Brad Pitt *(Interview With the Vampire)*

432. What is RuPaul's real first name?
   (a) Robert
   (b) Roy
   (c) Rock
   (d) RuPaul

433. What was Rock Hudson's real first name?
   (a) Robert
   (b) Roy

(c) Rock

(d) RuPaul

434. What was Divine's real first name?

(a) Henry

(b) Harold

(c) Harris

(d) Hector

Doug Savant

435. In which of the following films did Liberace make a cameo appearance?

(a) *The Loved One* (1965)

(b) *Advise and Consent* (1962)

(c) *Norman . . . Is That You?* (1976)

(d) *Can't Stop the Music* (1980)

436. What was the last film in which Marlene Dietrich appeared?

(a) *Judgment at Nuremberg*

(b) *Paris When It Sizzles*
(c) *Blazing Saddles*
(d) *Just a Gigolo*

437. Doug Savant portrays Matt Fielding, the gay character on *Melrose Place*. What is the actor's birthday?
(a) January 19
(b) June 21
(c) July 23
(d) December 25

ANT

438. Stand-up comic ANT (now his legal name—yes, all caps) plays Barry, a gay recurring character on WB's *Unhappily Ever After.* Prior to coming out, the comedian used to joke in his act about a fictitious girlfriend named . . .

  (a) Mindy
  (b) Mary
  (c) Marcy
  (d) Mercy

439. Who was quoted as saying, "When I got my first TV set, I stopped caring so much about having a close relationship"?

  (a) Quentin Crisp
  (b) Andy Warhol
  (c) Divine
  (d) Liberace

440. Lily Tomlin commented, "I remember seeing _____, and I just hated it. I didn't want to see a lesbian depicted that way. It was awful."

  (a) *The Killing of Sister George*
  (b) *Walk on the Wild Side*
  (c) *The Children's Hour*
  (d) *Cleopatra Jones*

441. Boy George described to the Associated Press an incident where he was allegedly beaten by bouncers at a London nightclub. Said Boy George, "They kicked me and punched me and broke my _____."

  (a) arm
  (b) finger
  (c) fingernails
  (d) platform shoes

442. Scott Thompson noted to the press, "I didn't have sex until I was _____ years old. And I survived. It didn't kill me. In fact, it gave me strength. I would advise that young gay guys don't have sex until they're a little older right now."
   (a) 23
   (b) 24
   (c) 25
   (d) 26

443. In his writings, who referred to a man as "the master-mistress of my passion"?
   (a) Jean Genet
   (b) Tennessee Williams
   (c) William Shakespeare
   (d) Paul Rudnick

444. Who was described by a columnist for London's *Daily Mirror* as "the summit of sex—the pinnacle of masculine, feminine, and neuter"?
   (a) Elton John
   (b) Boy George
   (c) Liberace
   (d) Eartha Kitt

445. Rupert Graves, star of the films *Different for Girls* and *Maurice,* formerly worked with a travelling circus as a . . .
   (a) clown
   (b) trapeze artist
   (c) lion trainer
   (d) costume designer

446. Who made the following statement? "I get offered so

many bad movies. And they're all raging queens or transvestites or Martians.''

(a) David Bowie

(b) Tim Curry

(c) Quentin Crisp

(d) Jaye Davidson

447. Liberace's last public performance was in 1986 at . . .

(a) Caesar's Palace

(b) Radio City Music Hall

(c) Carnegie Hall

(d) Hollywood Bowl

448. Who was described by a critic in the following way? "She has sex but no particular gender.''

(a) Annie Lennox

(b) Madonna

(c) Sandra Bernhard

(d) Marlene Dietrich

449. Claiming that a particular TV show played an important role in the history of the Village People, who made the following statement? "It was the kids on our show who first spelled out the letters YMCA with their arms and hands.''

(a) Mario Lopez talking about *Saved By the Bell*

(b) Dick Van Patten talking about *Eight Is Enough*

(c) Dick Clark talking about *American Bandstand*

(d) Pee Wee Herman talking about *Pee Wee's Playhouse*

450. Who commented on Ellen DeGeneres's coming out as a lesbian in the following way? "Everybody should be able to come out of whatever holes or closets or trunks they're in.''

(a) Laura Dern

(b) Glenn Close
(c) Judith Light
(d) Oprah Winfrey

451. Interviewed by Diane Sawyer on *Prime Time Live* immediately following the coming-out episode of *Ellen*, Ellen DeGeneres shared that she came out to her mother while walking on the beach in . . .
(a) North Carolina
(b) South Carolina
(c) Florida
(d) Mississippi

452. Tony Award-winning actress Cherry Jones *(The Heiress)* revealed that she knew she was gay because "she spent hours counting the freckles on _____'s face" pictured on the back of that singer's album cover.
(a) Janis Ian
(b) Joan Baez
(c) Julie Andrews
(d) Doris Day

453. Amy Ray of the Indigo Girls has _____ sisters who are also lesbian.
(a) two
(b) three
(c) four
(d) five

454. Who wrote a book titled *Take It Like A Man*?
(a) Boy George
(b) Ian McKellan
(c) Rupert Everett
(d) RuPaul

455. Who wrote a book titled *Lettin' It All Hang Out?*
    (a) Boy George
    (b) Ian McKellan
    (c) Rupert Everett
    (d) RuPaul

456. Who wrote a novel titled *Hello Darling, Are You Working?*
    (a) Boy George
    (b) Ian McKellan
    (c) Rupert Everett
    (d) RuPaul

457. Filmmaker Gregg Araki *(The Living End, Totally F***ed Up, The Doom Generation, Nowhere),* commented, "Just because a movie is gay or independent doesn't make it good. I'd rather see fucking _____ than see most of them."
    (a) *Coneheads*
    (b) *It's Pat*
    (c) *Wayne's World*
    (d) *The Sound of Music*

458. Divine appeared in several films directed by John Waters. Where did the two meet?
    (a) in high school
    (b) in college
    (c) in the Navy
    (d) in France

459. Director Gus Van Sant *(My Own Private Idaho)* directed a music video with . . .
    (a) The B-52's
    (b) Jimmy Somervile
    (c) Red Hot Chili Peppers
    (d) San Francisco's Gay Men's Chorus

460. Whose stage debut was a performance in drag at a Red Cross pageant?
   (a) Annie Lennox
   (b) Liza Minnelli
   (c) Marlene Dietrich
   (d) Quentin Crisp

461. Speaking about the *Ellen* coming-out episode, which cast member was quoted in *TV Guide* with the following statement? "For a lot of people, this was like Jackie Robinson in the major leagues. I feel like, in my tiny part, I kind of made a little television history."
   (a) Joely Fisher (Paige)
   (b) Jeremy Piven (Spence)
   (c) David Anthony Higgins (Joe)
   (d) Patrick Bristow (Peter)

14

Places . . .

Perhaps some thespians were *born* to play gay. Each of the very accomplished actors and actresses listed below has indeed played a memorable film or TV character (or two) who was gay or lesbian.

Match each of the actors/actresses (Column A) with his/her place of birth (Column B).

Column A

462. _____ Jane Alexander *(A Question of Love)*

463. _____ Joanna Cassidy *(The Laughing Policeman, Other Mothers)*

464. _____ Cher *(Silkwood)*

465. _____ Glenn Close *(Serving in Silence)*

466. _____ Jeff Daniels *(Fifth of July)*

Cher

467. _____ Bruce Davison *(Longtime Companion)*

468. _____ Whoopi Goldberg *(Boys on the Side)*

469. _____ Tom Hanks *(Philadelphia)*

470. _____ Hal Holbrook *(That Certain Summer)*

471. _____ William Hurt *(Kiss of the Spider Woman)*

472. _____ Kevin Kline *(In & Out)*

473. _____ Swoosie Kurtz *(Citizen Ruth)*

474. _____ Estelle Parsons *(Roseanne)*

475. _____ Eric Roberts *(It's My Party)*

476. _____ Gena Rowlands *(A Question of Love)*

477. _____ Tom Selleck *(In & Out)*

478. _____ Martin Sheen *(Consenting Adult, That Certain Summer)*

479. _____ Meryl Streep *(Manhattan)*

480. _____ Patrick Swayze *(To Wong Foo . . .)*

481. _____ Robin Williams *(The Birdcage)*

Column B

   (a)   Washington, D.C.
   (b)   Omaha, Nebr.
   (c)   Chicago
   (d)   Houston, Tex.
   (e)   Cleveland, Ohio
   (f)   Concord, Calif.
   (g)   Boston
   (h)   Athens, Ga.
   (i)   Philadelphia

(j) St. Louis

(k) Detroit

(l) Summit, N.J.

(m) Greenwich, Conn.

(n) El Centro, Calif.

(o) Cambria, Wis.

(p) Dayton, Ohio

(q) Marblehead, Mass.

(r) Camden, N.J.

(s) Biloxi, Miss.

(t) New York City

15

Miss Things

Circle the correct answer.

482. Jaye Davidson received an Academy Award nomination as Best Supporting Actor for *The Crying Game*. Additionally, the National Board of Review's D.W. Griffith Awards recognized Davidson by creating an entirely new category titled . . .
   (a) Best Supporting Actor/Actress Award
   (b) Best-Kept Secret Award
   (c) The Auspicious Debut Award
   (d) Best Full-Frontal Nudity Award

483. Which of the following actors was *not* nominated for a role performed in women's clothing?
   (a) Dustin Hoffman in *Tootsie*
   (b) John Lithgow in *The World According to Garp*
   (c) Robin Williams in *Mrs. Doubtfire*
   (d) Jack Lemon in *Some Like It Hot*

484. Who cross-dressed in the 1915 silent film *A Woman?*
   (a) Rudolph Valentino
   (b) Douglas Fairbanks
   (c) Charlie Chaplin
   (d) Gloria Swanson

485. In the 1993 film *National Lampoon's Loaded Weapon 1,* who appeared in drag as a Girl Scout?
   (a) Tim Conway
   (b) Tim Curry
   (c) Tom Selleck
   (d) Lily Tomlin

486. Explaining the inspiration for his role in *The Birdcage,* Nathan Lane quipped, "I did a young _____."
   (a) Lady Bird Johnson
   (b) Barbara Bush
   (c) Nancy Reagan
   (d) Eleanor Roosevelt

487. Drag star and gay porn director Chi Chi LaRue appeared in . . .
   (a) Madonna's "Deeper and Deeper" video
   (b) The Weather Girls' "It's Raining Men" video
   (c) RuPaul's "Supermodel" video
   (d) Richard Simmons's "Sweatin' to the Oldies" video

488. Depicting Howard Stern in drag, the paperback cover of *Miss America* is available in three different versions. What haircolor is *not* one of the choices?
   (a) blonde
   (b) red
   (c) brunette
   (d) black

Chi Chi LaRue

489. Videotaped at a Hilton hotel in Houston in 1985, *Dream Boys Review* was a beauty pageant featuring female impersonators. Who hosted the show?
  (a) Regis Philbin and Vicki Lawrence
  (b) Lyle Waggoner and Ruth Buzzi
  (c) Steve Allen and Jayne Meadows
  (d) Jack Lemmon and Tony Curtis

490. Which one of the Marx Brothers dressed in drag as a nurse in the 1931 film *Monkey Business*?
  (a) Chico

(b) Groucho
(c) Harpo
(d) Zeppo

491. Director Edward D. Wood Jr., who cross-dressed in real life, cast himself in the cross-dressing lead role in *Glen or Glenda?* (1953). What was his pseudonym as an actor?
(a) Daniel Davis
(b) Dee Dee Davis
(c) Zsa Zsa Davis
(d) Ann B. Davis

492. Who portrays Wood in the film *Ed Wood* (1994)?
(a) Johnny Depp
(b) Robert Downey, Jr.
(c) Bill Murray
(d) Chevy Chase

493. In *The Morning After* (1986), starring Jane Fonda, Frankie (James "Gypsy" Haake) explains, "Honey, I'm a drag queen, not a transvestite. I don't buy no _____."
(a) housedresses
(b) polyester
(c) plaids
(d) sensible shoes

494. In *Spit-Ball Sadie* (1915), a film about an all-women baseball team, Harold Lloyd portrays a female . . .
(a) pitcher
(b) catcher
(c) team manager
(d) umpire

495. In *The Rocky Horror Picture Show* (1976), Dr. Frank N.

Furter (Tim Curry) comes from a galaxy called Transsexual and a planet called . . .

(a) Fuchsia
(b) Hairdo
(c) Homo
(d) Transylvania

The Rocky Horror Picture Show

496. What's the name of the club where Dil (Jaye Davidson) sings in *The Crying Game* (1992)?

(a) The Borough
(b) The Cosmo
(c) The Metro
(d) The Underground

497. In *The Associate,* Laurel (Whoopi Goldberg) and a professional female impersonator named Charlie (Kenny Kerr) are friends. Dressed as Barbra Streisand, Charlie proclaims, "It's the new me! Am I not fabulous? . . . And does Babs

demand top dollar?! Honey, I'm making twice the amount of tips I made when I was doing _____ and Judy— may they rest in peace.''
  (a) Marilyn
  (b) Mae
  (c) Baby Jane Dexter
  (d) Mommie Dearest

498. In *Always Leave Them Laughing* (1949), who performs in drag as Carmen Miranda?
  (a) Milton Berle
  (b) Mickey Rooney
  (c) Danny Kaye
  (d) Bugs Bunny

499. In *Babes on Broadway* (1941), who performs in drag as Carmen Miranda?
  (a) Milton Berle
  (b) Mickey Rooney
  (c) Danny Kaye
  (d) Bugs Bunny

500. In *The Rose* (1979), Rose (Bette Midler) visits a gay bar where female impersonators perform. The drag show's MC (Michael Greer) imitates . . .
  (a) Carol Channing
  (b) Bette Davis
  (c) Ethel Merman
  (d) Tallulah Bankhead

501. Discussing mainstream films that feature drag queens as characters, who expressed the following opinion? ''I hate to see straight men playing drag queens to tell you the truth. You know, the cutting edge of drag is long gone, only because

now it's family-friendly. I think families should run for their lives when they see a drag queen, not cuddle up to them. I like different kinds of drag queens—psycho drag queens, drag queens with chain saws.''

(a) John Waters

(b) Gregg Araki

(c) Alexis Arquette

(d) Chi Chi LaRue

502. In *To Wong Foo . . .* , Noxema (Wesley Snipes) states, ''When a gay man has way too much _____, he is a drag queen.''

(a) fashion for one gender

(b) time on his hands

(c) foundation

(d) credit limit

In Print

Circle the correct answer.

503. On a 1993 cover of *Vanity Fair* magazine, a photo depicted Cindy Crawford shaving . . .
   (a) k.d. lang's face
   (b) k.d. lang's armpits
   (c) k.d. lang's legs
   (d) Harvey Fierstein's legs

504. Who appeared on the cover of the first issue of *Entertainment Weekly* in February of 1990?
   (a) Ellen DeGeneres
   (b) Elton John
   (c) k.d. lang
   (d) Jodie Foster

505. An *Entertainment Weekly* cover proclaimed, "_____
IS NOT A LESBIAN . . . BUT SHE PLAYS ONE ON TV."
   (a) Morgan Fairchild *(Roseanne)*
   (b) Amanda Donohue *(L.A. Law)*
   (c) Nora Dunn *(Sisters)*
   (d) Laura Dern *(Ellen)*

506. Who came out in the June 2, 1992, issue of *The Advocate?*
   (a) k.d. lang
   (b) Sandra Bernhard
   (c) Amanda Bearse
   (d) Chastity Bono

507. In what publication did Melissa Etheridge discuss her Kansas hometown with the following remark? "Poor Leavenworth. They're known for a prison and the most famous homosexual."
   (a) *The Advocate*
   (b) *Out*
   (c) *Curve*
   (d) *The Des Moines Register*

508. In January 1997, in what magazine did David Bowie discuss his "dodgy past" as a bisexual in the following way? "I guess I've been heterosexual for so many years that most of the people I know have known me only . . . as 'the straight guy.' "
   (a) *Entertainment Weekly*
   (b) *Vanity Fair*
   (c) *Details*
   (d) *Anything That Moves*

509. In November 1996, what magazine cover pictured Melissa Etheridge and Julie Cypher with the headline, "WE'RE HAVING A BABY"?

(a) *Time*

(b) *Newsweek*

(c) *People*

(d) *Girlfriends*

510. On the cover of an April 1997 *Advocate,* what event was dubbed "The Gay Super Bowl"?

(a) the Tony Awards

(b) the Grammy Awards

(c) the Academy Awards

(d) VH-1's Fashion Awards

511. In July 1996, what magazine included a photo of Elton John "and his beau" at a fashion show?

(a) *People*

(b) *Us*

(c) *Vanity Fair*

(d) *GQ*

512. Prior to playing Frankie in the film *Kiss Me, Guido,* Nick Scotti appeared as the male example of "The Biology of Beauty" for a cover story in . . .

(a) *Time*

(b) *Newsweek*

(c) *Details*

(d) *Genre*

513. In July 1997, to what publication did Rupert Everett offer the following statement? "If I am typecast [as a result

of playing gay roles], then I am. I don't have any illusions about it. My feeling is that if I only get to play gay characters from now on, then that's really fine by me. Gay characters, contrary to popular opinion, are not all the same."

   (a) *The New York Times*
   (b) *The New York Post*
   (c) *The Village Voice*
   (d) *Homo X-tra*

514. In 1968, what publication reported, "Unashamedly queer characters are everywhere!"?

   (a) *Time*
   (b) *Newsweek*
   (c) *Life*
   (d) *The Catholic Film Newsletter*

515. The novel *The Front Runner*, about an Olympics runner and his love affair with his coach, was originally optioned for the screen by Paul Newman, who intended to play the coach. To what magazine did Newman make the following statement in 1967? "I'm not ready for a cop-out. I won't tolerate this project being turned into a watered-down love story, or substituting a female for the runner as has been suggested by people who should know better."

   (a) *Variety*
   (b) *The Los Angeles Times*
   (c) *The New York Times*
   (d) *Blueboy*

516. In a 1997 issue, *TV Guide* listed their picks of the "100

Greatest Episodes of All Time.'' What number did the *Ellen* coming-out episode place?

    (a) 45

    (b) 35

    (c) 25

    (d) 15

A Very Good Year

Circle the correct answer.

517. In what year was actor and gay activist Sir Ian McKellen knighted?
- (a) 1989
- (b) 1991
- (c) 1993
- (d) 1995

518. Gay model Dirk Shafer, star of his own "mockumentary" titled *Man of the Year,* was *Playgirl*'s Centerfold of the Year in . . .
- (a) 1988
- (b) 1990
- (c) 1992
- (d) 1994

Dirk Shafer and Phil Donahue

519. Accepting the New Music Award for Folk album of the Year (for which Tracy Chapman, the Indigo Girls, and Phranc had also been nominated), Michelle Shocked quipped, "This category should have been called 'Best Lesbian Vocalist.'" In what year did Michelle Shocked win the award?
   (a) 1985
   (b) 1987
   (c) 1989
   (d) 1991

520. In what year did *The Times of Harvey Milk* win the Academy Award for Best Documentary?
   (a) 1983
   (b) 1985
   (c) 1987
   (d) 1989

521. In what year did Ellen DeGeneres win the Showtime's Funniest Person in America award?
  (a) 1982
  (b) 1984
  (c) 1986
  (d) 1988

522. In what year did the dramatic series *N.Y.P.D.* become the first television series to portray homosexuals?
  (a) 1967
  (b) 1969
  (c) 1971
  (d) 1973

523. In what year did Mart Crowley's *Boys in the Band* open off-Broadway?
  (a) 1964
  (b) 1966
  (c) 1968
  (d) 1970

524. *CBS Presents: The Homosexuals,* hosted by Mike Wallace, aired in . . .
  (a) 1963
  (b) 1965
  (c) 1967
  (d) 1969

525. According to a *Rolling Stone* profile on Elton John, what year did the singer meet lyricist Bernie Taupin?
  (a) 1963
  (b) 1965
  (c) 1967
  (d) 1969

526. What model year is the Cadillac convertible driven in *To Wong Foo* . . . ?
   (a) 1963
   (b) 1965
   (c) 1967
   (d) 1969

527. In *Bound,* what model year is Corky's Chevy truck?
   (a) 1963
   (b) 1965
   (c) 1967
   (d) 1969

528. In *Set It Off,* what model year is Cleo's Chevy Impala?
   (a) 1962
   (b) 1964
   (c) 1966
   (d) 1968

529. Paul Lynde made his Broadway debut in a revue titled *New Faces of* _____, which also featured Eartha Kitt and Alice Ghostley.
   (a) *1952*
   (b) *1954*
   (c) *1956*
   (d) *1958*

Paul Lynde

530. Sir John Gielgud, a longtime vocal supporter of gay rights, was born in . . .
  (a) 1898
  (b) 1900
  (c) 1902
  (d) 1904

Bad Vibes

Circle the correct answer.

531. In an episode of the 1970s sitcom *All in the Family,* Archie Bunker discovered that a friend of his was gay. *The Advocate* magazine reported that someone "happened to tune in to this episode . . . and was shocked and disgusted, since he didn't think this was a subject to be seen in the polite company of his family." Who was this shocked and disgusted TV viewer?
- (a) Richard Nixon
- (b) Billy Graham
- (c) Pat Boone
- (d) Michael Jackson

532. Appearing on *Fox News Sunday* in the fall of 1996, who reacted to the speculation that *Ellen* would feature a lesbian star by making the following comment? "I find it hard to believe because she's so popular. She's such an attractive actress."

   (a) Pat Robertson
   (b) Pat Buchanan
   (c) Newt Gingrich
   (d) Janet Reno

533. To what group of people did radio host Rush Limbaugh say, "Take your deadly, sickly behavior and keep it to yourselves"?

   (a) celebrities who raise funds for AIDS charities
   (b) AIDS activists who demonstrated at St. Patrick's Cathedral
   (c) the cast of *Angels in America*
   (d) the cast of *Victor/Victoria*

534. Speaking at an event in Des Moines, Iowa, sponsored by the National Campaign to Protect the Sanctity of Marriage, syndicated radio host Jay Sekulow opined, "If same-sex marriages are legalized, it will _____."

   (a) confuse children
   (b) lead to drag queens as flower girls
   (c) be the end of normal bachelor parties
   (d) be the end of our culture

535. What film includes the following disclaimer? "This film is not intended as an indictment of the homosexual world. It is set in one small segment of that world, which is not meant to be representative of the whole."

(a) *Silence of the Lambs*
(b) *Cruising*
(c) *Claire of the Moon*
(d) *Can't Stop the Music*

19

Best Friends

Below is a list of quotes (Column A), followed by a list of celebrated women (Column B). Match each woman with the correct quote.

Column A

536. _____ "I'm the ultimate fag hag. I'm the fat girl who took you to the prom and let you come out as we slow-danced to 'Lean on Me'—the Club Nouveau version."

537. _____ "I've dated many a man who now has a boy-friend."

538. _____ "I dated all the boys who were homosexual. I liked them better. They weren't fresh."

539. _____ "I'm not the least bit gay . . . but my girlfriend is."

540. _____ "Homosexuals make the best friends because they care about you as a woman and are not jealous. They love you but don't try to screw up your head."

541. _____ "I can say to my gay friends 'Men are shits,' and they agree. It's a kind of sisterhood in a way."

542. _____ "My gay audience is as important to me as my pumps. Just as I don't feel whole unless I have on five-inch pumps, I don't feel whole unless I have a gay crowd."

543. _____ "Without homosexuals there would be no Hollywood, no theatre, no arts."

Column B

- (a) Margaret Cho
- (b) Deborah Gibson
- (c) Bianca Jagger
- (d) Patti LaBelle
- (e) Sarah Jessica Parker
- (f) Dolly Parton
- (g) Debbie Reynolds
- (h) Elizabeth Taylor

Speaking Out

Below is a list of quotes (Column A), followed by a list of actors/actresses, musicians, and stand-up comics (Column B). Match each performer with the correct quote.

Column A

544. _____ "I didn't all of a sudden feel, *I'm gay*—I just all of a sudden felt, *Oh, I love.*"

545. _____ "It's the visibility of gay and lesbian performers that really reaches people's hearts, and it allows them to be open to accepting us."

546. _____ "I'm not someone who sets [myself] up as an icon of sexual orientation. But my private life has never been a secret."

547. _____ "Most people do think of me as just another pinko faggot, a bleeding heart, a do-gooder. But that's what I am."

548. _____ "I can't represent anyone but myself. I make that as clear as I can as often as I can. Nobody elected me to this position. You'd like to make everybody proud and happy, but it can't be done. Even Mary Tyler Moore can't represent all single women."

549. _____ "It's hard to justify having worked for black civil rights in the '60s and not work for my own civil rights in the '90s."

550. _____ "We jump so much to make it an onus that someone hasn't come out. Maybe it's not a big thing to those people. Maybe it's not an issue."

551. _____ "I've had long-term sexual relationships with both men and women. If that classifies me as a bisexual, then I'm a bisexual. I'm very committed to people, so when I'm with somebody, I'm with them."

552. _____ "I've traveled, but I would not say I'm gay. I suppose if someone had to use a label . . . I've had a bisexual life."

553. _____ "I like the idea that people are sexual without having to attach prefixes."

554. _____ "Everyone is more or less bisexual. People just don't want to admit it."

555. _____ "I like them all—men I mean. And a few chicks now and then."

556. _____ "As a former teacher, I know that you need to repeat things and repeat things, and you need to say it in a bunch of different ways until everyone finally hears it: that's it's okay to be gay and to come out."

557. _____ "Some people look at us as spawn of Satan, some people look at us as role models."

558. _____ "We need to quit bitching at each other. That's gotta end. If we [within the gay and lesbian community] spent as much time yelling at the government as we spend yelling at each other, we'd already have our rights."

559. _____ "Everybody in their own time. When people are out, straight people see them as representing the whole community. So let them do it when they're ready. If we drag them kicking and screaming out of the closet, they won't be heroes."

560. _____ "You think there's some big black hole you're going to fall into and that all of a sudden people who have loved you all your life aren't going to love you anymore. And I'm here to tell you that that does not happen."

561. _____ "My being openly homosexual doesn't appear to have damaged my career in any way. That fact might offer encouragement to anyone who's still nervous of exiting the closet."

562. _____ "I can walk into a room, onto a set, into a meeting without feeling 'less than' because of this *secret*. There is a

power that one gains by being honest that is not easy to measure.''

563. _____ ''I was thinking, what's the thing anyone could ask me now or say about me? And it's like nothing, really. I mean, not even Howard Stern can hurt me now.''

564. _____ ''Until [I came out], the only thing I felt expert in was theatre. Now I realize I have another expertise, and source of pride: my sexuality.''

Anne Heche and Ellen DeGeneres

565. _____ "It's like, I want to be out. I want to be out!"

566. _____ "I'm not a very good liar."

567. _____ "I just wish more of my fellow queers would come out. It's nice out here."

568. _____ "Surprise, middle America! Not all gay people are the same."

569. _____ "The ice has been broken. We are in every job, we're every color. We're not out to take over the world. We just want to live in it."

Column B

   (a) Mitchell Anderson

   (b) Joan Baez

   (c) Amanda Bearse

   (d) Andy Bell (*Erasure*)

   (e) Sandra Bernhard

   (f) Leonard Bernstein

   (g) Dan Butler

   (h) Simon Callow

   (i) Kate Clinton

   (j) Ellen DeGeneres

   (k) Lea DeLaria

   (l) Rupert Everett

 (m) Melissa Etheridge

   (n) Harvey Fierstein

   (o) Nigel Hawthorne

   (p) Anne Heche

   (q) Janis Ian

   (r) Elton John

(s) k.d. lang

(t) Sir Ian McKellen

(u) Sal Mineo

Sal Mineo

(v) Andy Ray (Indigo Girls)

(w) Ron Romanovsky (Romanovsky & Phillips)

(x) Jill Sobule

(y) Michael Stipe (R.E.M.)

(z) Suzanne Westenhoefer

Answers

"Now At a Video Store Near You"

1. (b) a car rental clerk
2. (b) Archie and Jughead
3. (c) decorates his room
4. (d) *Ladybugs* starring Rodney Dangerfield
5. (b) Judy Garland and Liberace
6. (b) Robert Goulet and Cher
7. (b) 12
8. (b) "She's butch."
9. (c) *Addams Family Values*
10. (b) *Wayne's World 2*
11. (d) a Catholic
12. (b) *Oedipus Rex*
13. (a) *Male Call*
14. (c) *G-String*
15. (d) *Erasure*
16. (c) *Body of Evidence*
17. (c) "I Say a Little Prayer"
18. (b) "Piece of My Heart"
19. (a) coffee
20. (c) 5
21. (d) Tom Jones

22. (c) Grace Jones
23. (a) Patrick Swayze
24. (d) Andrew Dice Clay
25. (c) with a hustler
26. (a) Chicago
27. (c) Wallace High
28. (b) organic pasta
29. (b) Sister Boy
30. (b) B+
31. (b) Glenn Close
32. (b) Greenleaf
33. (d) "I Will Survive"
34. (a) Randy Becker
35. (b) Peter and Sal
36. (c) condoms
37. (d) festive
38. (c) *The Village Voice*
39. (c) the Bronx
40. (b) Money
41. (b) Nathan Leopold, Jr.
42. (d) *Protocol*
43. (c) *Revenge of the Nerds*
44. (a) Marcia
45. (c) Noreen
46. (d) Kristy McNichol
47. (c) *It's Just Sex*
48. (b) Kevin Nealon
49. (c) florist
50. (d) William Baldwin
51. (c) men
52. (c) Scorpio
53. (d) Sagittarius
54. (a) *B-Boy Blues*
55. (d) Powders

56. (c) Churchill's Launderette
57. (a) *Annie Hall*
58. (d) drapes
59. (b) red lingerie
60. (d) Dorothy
61. (c) a freedom-ring necklace
62. (b) West Virginia
63. (a) faces to paint
64. (d) Aunt Jack
65. (b) an agent
66. (a) actor
67. (a) Best Actress
68. (c) Hollywood
69. (d) BAD GIRL
70. (a) HONK IF YOU'RE HORNY
71. (a) Philadelphia Eagles
72. (b) Jan
73. (d) "I've Never Been to Me"
74. (c) "We Are Family"
75. (a) STRAIGHT ACTING
76. (a) Superman
77. (d) PSYCHO BITCH
78. (b) TIGHT BUTTS DRIVE ME NUTS
79. (b) furniture
80. (b) raining
81. (d) *Falling Down*
82. (b) *Crocodile Dundee II*
83. (d) David Bowie
84. (b) John Larroquette
85. (a) Camille
86. (a) Albert
87. (b) The China Palace
88. (b) 1069
89. (b) 4

90. (b) 3S
91. (a) Rent-A-Heap
92. (c) George Carlin
93. (d) Nathan Lane
94. (a) dress
95. (c) Attitude
96. (b) *All Over Me*
97. (d) Gay Bruce
98. (d) Jodie Foster
99. (d) everything
100. (c) Ricki Lake
101. (c) Mariel Hemingway
102. (d) on Fire Island
103. (c) Todd Tomorrow
104. (a) Dustin Hoffman
105. (a) Gareth
106. (c) 15
107. (b) Roddy McDowall
108. (c) Mama Cass
109. (b) 12
110. (d) Luther's
111. (c) 7th
112. (a) sailor
113. (c) cop

Celluloid Scrapbook

114. (b) Candice Bergen
115. (b) *Love and Death*
116. (c) Rue McClanahan
117. (c) Treat Williams
118. (c) Rita Moreno
119. (b) *The Way We Were*

120. (c) her son's football sweatshirt
121. (b) the Navy
122. (d) Frank Sinatra
123. (d) the sugarplum fairies
124. (c) David Bowie
125. (d) *Sleeper*
126. (d) a brothel in New Orleans
127. (d) a brothel in New Orleans
128. (b) your mascara
129. (d) Levi's
130. (a) Bruce Dern
131. (d) *Cleopatra Jones and the Casino of Gold*
132. (a) hairstylists
133. (b) *The Gay Brothers*
134. (c) the Cherry Sisters
135. (c) Beach Boy
136. (c) Rachel Roberts
137. (d) Faggot
138. (c) *A Very Natural Thing*
139. (a) "My hero!"
140. (c) Pinky
141. (d) Mr. Joyboy
142. (d) Doris Day
143. (b) Bette Davis

Film Quotes

144. (c) Janeane Garofalo to Steve Zahn in *Reality Bites*
145. (c) Steven Weber in *Jeffrey*
146. (b) Sharon Stone in *Basic Instinct*
147. (a) Kevin Bacon in *JFK*
148. (b) Anita Gilette in *Boys on the Side*
149. (c) Robin Williams in *The Birdcage*

150. (c) Michael Ontkean in *Making Love*
151. (a) Kevin Kline in *In & Out*
152. (a) Jason Flemyng in *Alive & Kicking*
153. (a) Antonio Fargas in *Car Wash*
154. (a) Rock Hudson to Doris Day in *Pillow Talk*
155. (b) Charles Pierce in *Torch Song Trilogy*
156. (b) Guinevere Turner to V.S. Brodie in *Go Fish*
157. (c) Richard Gere in *American Gigolo*
158. (b) Stephen Baldwin to Josh Charles in *Threesome*
159. (d) Lily Tomlin in *Flirting With Disaster*
160. (b) Isaiah Washington in *Get on the Bus*
161. (b) Mary-Louise Parker in *Longtime Companion*
162. (c) Peter Friedman in *Single White Female*
163. (b) Jennifer Dundas in *The First Wives Club*
164. (a) James Garner in *Victor/Victoria*
165. (b) James Remar in *Boys on the Side*
166. (b) Alfred Molina in *Prick Up Your Ears*
167. (a) River Phoenix to Keanu Reeves in *My Own Private Idaho*
168. (c) Gene Hackman to Dan Futterman in *The Birdcage*
169. (c) James Coco in *Only When I Laugh*
170. (b) Shirley MacLaine in *Postcards from the Edge*
171. (a) Joan Cusack in *In & Out*
172. (c) Peter Sellers in *Revenge of the Pink Panther*
173. (a) Perry King in *A Different Story*
174. (a) Richard Jenkins in *Flirting With Disaster*
175. (a) Keanu Reeves to River Phoenix in *My Own Private Idaho*
176. (c) T. Wendy McMill in *Go Fish*
177. (b) Adam Nathan to Steven Buscemi in *Parting Glances*
178. (a) Janeane Garofalo to Winona Ryder in *Reality Bites*
179. (c) Josh Charles in *Threesome*
180. (c) Robert Beltran in *Scenes from the Class Struggle in Beverly Hills*

181. (b) Matthew Broderick to Harvey Fierstein in *Torch Song Trilogy*
182. (b) Stephen Baldwin to Josh Charles in *Threesome*
183. (b) Jack Thompson to Russell Crowe in *The Sum of Us*
184. (c) Guinevere Turner in *Go Fish*
185. (b) Laura Flynn Boyle to Josh Charles in *Threesome*
186. (a) Michael York in *Cabaret*
187. (c) Harvey Fierstein in *Torch Song Trilogy*
188. (b) Terence Stamp in *The Adventures of Priscilla, Queen of the Desert*
189. (c) Mary-Louise Parker in *Boys on the Side*
190. (b) Diane Keaton in *The First Wives Club*
191. (c) Mel Brooks in *To Be Or Not to Be*
192. (c) Stephen Baldwin in *Threesome*
193. (c) Ben Affleck in *Chasing Amy*
194. (c) Richard Jenkins to Josh Brolin in *Flirting With Disaster*
195. (b) Terence Stamp in *The Adventures of Priscilla, Queen of the Desert*
196. (a) Rex Reed in *Myra Breckinridge*
197. (c) Barbara Stanwyck in *Walk on the Wild Side*
198. (a) Mariel Hemingway in *Personal Best*
199. (c) Bronson Pinchot in *It's My Party*
200. (b) Harry Hamlin in *Making Love*
201. (a) Rupert Everett in *Another Country*
202. (a) Andre Braucher in *Get on the Bus*
203. (c) Laurence Luckinbill in *Boys in the Band*
204. (c) Swoosie Kurtz to Mary Kay Place in *Citizen Ruth*
205. (a) Patricia Charbonneau to Helen Shaver in *Desert Hearts*
206. (a) Simon Callow in *Four Weddings and a Funeral*
207. (c) RuPaul in *A Very Brady Sequel*

A Kiss Is Just a Kiss

208. (f) Sara Gilbert
209. (b) Sammi Davis
210. (a) Bibi Anderson
211. (j) Elizabeth Young
212. (e) Patricia Donnelly
213. (i) Samantha MacLachlan
214. (d) Catherine Deneuve
215. (h) Helen Mirren
216. (c) Maria de Medeiros
217. (g) Lee Grant
218. *Poison Ivy*
219. *The Rainbow*
220. *Twice a Woman*
221. *Queen Christina*
222. *Personal Best*
223. *Set It Off*
224. *The Hunger*
225. *Losing Chase*
226. *Henry & June*
227. *The Balcony*
228. (g) Eusebio Poncella
229. (e) Brian Kerwin
230. (h) Campbell Scott
231. (c) John Dossett
232. (j) James Wilby
233. (d) Murray Head
234. (k) Michael York
235. (b) Divine
236. (f) John Lone
237. (i) Tom Selleck
238. (a) Michael Caine
239. *The Law of Desire*

240. *Torch Song Trilogy*
241. *Longtime Companion*
242. *Longtime Companion*
243. *Something for Everyone*
244. *Sunday Bloody Sunday*
245. *Maurice*
246. *Polyester*
247. *M. Butterfly*
248. *In & Out*
249. *Deathtrap*

Bar Hopping, Hollywood Style

250. (i) *Some of My Best Friends Are . . .*
251. (g) *Police Academy*
252. (b) *The Associate*
253. (h) *The Laughing Policeman*
254. (j) *P.J.*
255. (d) *Bar Girls*
256. (a) *Chasing Amy*
257. (f) *Torch Song Trilogy*
258. (e) *Wayne's World 2*
259. (c) *Bound*

Ellen's "Yep, I'm Gay" Episode

260. (e) David Anthony Higgins (Joe)
261. (h) Steven Eckholdt (Richard)
262. (b) Joely Fisher (Paige)
263. (k) Billy Bob Thornton
264. (a) Ellen DeGeneres (Ellen Morgan)
265. (o) Melissa Etheridge

266. (m) Gina Gershon
267. (c) Jeremy Piven (Spence)
268. (l) Demi Moore
269. (d) Clea Lewis (Audrey)
270. (j) Oprah Winfrey (Therapist)
271. (f) Patrick Bristow (Peter)
272. (n) Dwight Yoakam
273. (g) Laura Dern (Susan)
274. (i) k.d. lang (Janine)

TV Laugh Tracks

275. (a) choreographers
276. (b) bought myself a *Playboy*
277. (b) the fruit
278. (c) a football player
279. (b) a college newspaper
280. (b) Luke Perry
281. (d) Ted Danson
282. (a) the officiant
283. (d) Miles
284. (d) he climbed out on a window ledge
285. (a) Martha Stewart
286. (b) *Cybill*
287. (a) *Frasier*
288. (a) a drag queen
289. (a) a drag queen
290. (b) ''I Will Survive''
291. (c) $250
292. (d) religious-right protestors
293. (b) Norm Crosby
294. (b) Jackie (Laurie Metcalf)
295. (c) almost fainted

296. (c) Liza Minnelli
297. (b) Harry Shearer
298. (b) John Waters
299. (b) a gay purse snatcher
300. (b) cousin
301. (d) Richard Roundtree
302. (c) sports commentator
303. (b) Tony (Tony Danza)
304. (c) Tony Randall
305. (d) Harvey Fierstein
306. (a) Dorothy (Bea Arthur)
307. (d) Midge
308. (b) Trevor
309. (c) Harvey Fierstein
310. (b) cousin
311. (a) Birmingham, Alabama

TV Drama Queens

312. (b) Art Fleming (original *Jeopardy*)
313. (a) Charles Pierce
314. (b) a lesbian dental assistant
315. (d) first
316. (a) see a psychiatrist
317. (a) still a man
318. (d) in bed after sex
319. (a) a bed-and-breakfast
320. (b) Rue McClanahan
321. (b) Al Corey
322. (b) Donna Mills
323. (a) he had two lesbian mothers
324. (a) history teacher
325. (d) *All My Children*

326. (c) *General Hospital*
327. (d) Jim Carrey
328. (b) *Policewoman*
329. (b) Lorna Luft
330. (b) Vanessa Redgrave
331. (a) Lynn Redgrave
332. (d) Julie Andrews
333. (b) Vanessa Redgrave
334. (b) 34
335. (b) Brad Davis
336. (d) Ricky
337. (b) violin
338. (b) a six-part series
339. (b) *N.Y.P.D. Blue*
340. (d) guns

Talking Heads

341. (d) a ten-pound gay nose
342. (a) RuPaul
343. (c) comic Suzanne Westenhoefer
344. (c) a big dyke
345. (a) their mouth was full of one
346. (d) Dennis Rodman
347. (a) Geraldo Rivera
348. (d) "But, darling, what difference does it *make* as long as you look fabulous?"
349. (a) *20/20*
350. (c) Queens
351. (d) Tom Snyder
352. (b) *Geraldo*
353. (d) death defying
354. (c) Whoopi Goldberg

355. (b) David Lettermam
356. (a) Jay Leno

Channel Surfing

357. (a) ABC and CBS
358. (c) USA Network
359. (a) HBO
360. (c) NBC
361. (c) NBC
362. (a) PBS
363. (c) Showtime
364. (c) HBO
365. (c) NBC
366. (c) NBC
367. (a) ABC
368. (b) Showtime
369. (a) Comedy Central

Musical Notes

370. (d) Pansy Division
371. (d) Sappho
372. (d) choir
373. (c) 40
374. (c) Dusty Springfield
375. (d) Jill Sobule
376. (a) Bronski Beat
377. (d) Boy George
378. (b) Bruce Springsteen
379. (a) ''Bohemian Rhapsody''
380. (b) a Gym Teacher

381. (b) the Indigo Girls
382. (a) *Donahue*
383. (b) "Express Yourself"

Center Stage

384. (b) *Jeffrey*
385. (d) Estelle Getty
386. (d) Nathan Lane
387. (b) puke
388. (c) Robert Morse
389. (a) Anthony Perkins
390. (b) Mick Jagger
391. (c) Rex Chandler
392. (c) Dan Butler (from *Frasier*)
393. (c) Lord Laurence Olivier
394. (b) Frederic in *The Sound of Music*
395. (c) a Gun
396. (a) Nathan Lane
397. (d) Hamlet in *Hamlet*

People

398. (c) Richard Gere and Cindy Crawford
399. (b) Jean Claude Van Damme
400. (b) Michael Jackson
401. (d) Sigourney Weaver
402. (d) Mr. Lesbian
403. (a) a TV weatherman in Chicago
404. (b) Lou Diamond Phillips
405. (b) the 1993 Triangle Ball in Washington, D.C.
406. (b) drama teacher

407. (c) Zsa Zsa Gabor
408. (b) Whoopi Goldberg in *Boys on the Side*
409. (c) Shirley MacLaine in *The Children's Hour*
410. (a) Queens
411. (c) Leonard Maltin
412. (c) bitch
413. (c) *The Los Angeles Times*
414. (d) live in shame and embarrassment
415. (a) a dog
416. (d) Julia Roberts
417. (d) 62%
418. (b) Rosie O'Donnell
419. (c) Dick Dietrick on *Nightstand*
420. (c) England
421. (c) Rex Reed
422. (d) a hit
423. (c) the Bronx
424. (a) Peter Finch
425. (a) *Giant* (1956)
426. (a) *Cheech & Chong's Nice Dreams*
427. (a) Harry Hamlin to Michael Ontkean in *Making Love* (1982)
428. (b) Bette Midler
429. (d) Steve Martin
430. (c) Mae West
431. (a) Bonnie Hunt (*Jerry Maguire*)
432. (d) RuPaul
433. (b) Roy
434. (c) Harris
435. (a) *The Loved One* (1965)
436. (d) *Just a Gigolo*
437. (b) June 21
438. (c) Marcy
439. (b) Andy Warhol

440. (a) *The Killing of Sister George*
441. (c) fingernails
442. (b) 24
443. (c) William Shakespeare
444. (c) Liberace
445. (a) clown
446. (a) David Bowie
447. (b) Radio City Music Hall
448. (d) Marlene Dietrich
449. (c) Dick Clark talking about *American Bandstand*
450. (b) Glenn Close
451. (d) Mississippi
452. (c) Julie Andrews
453. (a) two
454. (a) Boy George
455. (d) RuPaul
456. (c) Rupert Everett
457. (a) *Coneheads*
458. (a) in high school
459. (c) Red Hot Chili Peppers
460. (c) Marlene Dietrich
461. (c) David Anthony Higgins (Joe)

Places

462. (g) Boston
463. (r) Camden, N.J.
464. (n) El Centro, Calif.
465. (m) Greenwich, Conn.
466. (h) Athens, Ga.
467. (i) Philadelphia
468. (t) New York City
469. (f) Concord, Calif.

470. (e) Cleveland, Ohio
471. (a) Washington, D.C.
472. (j) St. Louis
473. (b) Omaha, Nebr.
474. (q) Marblehead, Mass.
475. (s) Biloxi, Miss.
476. (o) Cambria, Wis.
477. (k) Detroit
478. (p) Dayton, Ohio
479. (l) Summit, N.J.
480. (d) Houston, Tex.
481. (c) Chicago

Miss Things

482. (c) The Auspicious Debut Award
483. (c) Robin Williams in *Mrs. Doubtfire*
484. (c) Charlie Chaplin
485. (b) Tim Curry
486. (b) Barbara Bush
487. (a) Madonna's ''Deeper and Deeper'' video
488. (d) black
489. (b) Lyle Waggoner and Ruth Buzzi
490. (c) Harpo
491. (a) Daniel Davis
492. (a) Johnny Depp
493. (a) housedresses
494. (a) pitcher
495. (d) Transylvania
496. (c) The Metro
497. (a) Marilyn
498. (a) Milton Berle
499. (b) Mickey Rooney

500. (b) Bette Davis
501. (a) John Waters
502. (a) fashion for one gender

In Print

503. (a) k.d. lang's face
504. (c) k.d. lang
505. (d) Laura Dern *(Ellen)*
506. (a) k.d. lang
507. (d) *The Des Moines Register*
508. (a) *Entertainment Weekly*
509. (b) *Newsweek*
510. (c) the Academy Awards
511. (a) *People*
512. (b) *Newsweek*
513. (b) *The New York Post*
514. (a) *Time*
515. (d) *Blueboy*
516. (b) 35

A Very Good Year

517. (b) 1991
518. (c) 1992
519. (c) 1989
520. (b) 1985
521. (a) 1982
522. (a) 1967
523. (c) 1968
524. (c) 1967
525. (c) 1967

526. (c) 1967
527. (a) 1963
528. (a) 1962
529. (a) *1952*
530. (d) 1904

Bad Vibes

531. (a) Richard Nixon
532. (a) Pat Robertson
533. (b) AIDS activists who demonstrated at St. Patrick's Cathedral
534. (d) be the end of our culture
535. (b) *Cruising*

Best Friends

536. (a) Margaret Cho
537. (b) Deborah Gibson
538. (g) Debbie Reynolds
539. (f) Dolly Parton
540. (c) Bianca Jagger
541. (e) Sarah Jessica Parker
542. (d) Patti LaBelle
543. (h) Elizabeth Taylor

Speaking Out

544. (p) Anne Heche
545. (w) Ron Romanovsky (Romanovsky & Phillips)
546. (o) Nigel Hawthorne
547. (f) Leonard Bernstein

548. (n) Harvey Fierstein
549. (q) Janis Ian
550. (g) Dan Butler
551. (e) Sandra Bernhard
552. (x) Jill Sobule
553. (y) Michael Stipe (R.E.M.)
554. (b) Joan Baez
555. (u) Sal Mineo
556. (i) Kate Clinton
557. (v) Amy Ray (Indigo Girls)
558. (k) Lea DeLaria
559. (z) Suzanne Westenhoefer
560. (m) Melissa Etheridge
561. (h) Simon Callow
562. (a) Mitchell Anderson
563. (j) Ellen DeGeneres
564. (t) Sir Ian McKellen
565. (s) k.d. lang
566. (d) Andy Bell (Erasure)
567. (r) Elton John
568. (l) Rupert Everett
569. (c) Amanda Bearse

Photo Credits

Rupert Everett
Photo courtesy: Wolf-Kasteller Public Relations

Boys on the Side
Photo courtesy: Archive Photos

The World According to Garp
Photo courtesy: Archive Photos

RuPaul
Photo courtesy: World of Wonder
Photo by: Albert Sanchez

Guinevere Turner
Photo courtesy: Evergreen Entertainment

Michael Greer
Photo courtesy: Michael Greer

Susan Sarandon in *The Hunger*
Photo courtesy: Fotos International / Archive Photos

Christopher Reeve in *Deathtrap*
Photo courtesy: Fotos International / Archive Photos

Ellen DeGeneres and Laura Dern
Photo courtesy: Archive Photos
Photo by: Reuters/ Mike Ansell

Estelle Parsons in *Roseanne*
Photo courtesy: Paramount Pictures / Archive Photos

Billy Crystal
Photo courtesy: Archive Photos

Amanda Bearse in *Married . . . With Children*
Photo courtesy: Fotos International / Archive Photos

Amanda Donohue in *L.A. Law*
Photo courtesy: Fotos International / Archive Photos

Wilson Cruz
Photo courtesy: Lighthouse Entertainment

Kate Clinton
Photo courtesy: Kate Clinton
Photo by: Joe Henson

Mario Lopez and Greg Louganis
Photo courtesy: USA Network
Photo by: Michael Grecco

Suzanne Westenhoefer
Photo courtesy: Judy Dlugacz, A Management and
Development Company
Photo by: Glenn Jussen

Indigo Girls
Photo courtesy: Epic
Photo by: Michael Halsband
© 1997 Sony Music

Men Out Loud
Photo courtesy: Mercury Records
Photo by: Tom Bianchi 1997

Madame Dish (a.k.a. Steven J. McCarthy) & Her Naughty
Boys
Photo courtesy: Madame Dish Productions, Inc.
© 1995 MDP

Lea DeLaria
Photo by: Ed Karvoski, Jr.

Sandra Bernhard, Candace Gingrich and Melissa
Etheridge (at GLAAD Media Awards)
Photo courtesy: Archive Photos
Photo by: Reuters / Groshong

Doug Savant of *Melrose Place*
Photo Courtesy: Fotos International/Archive Photos
Photo by: Dana Fineman

ANT
Photo courtesy: ANT
Photo by: Bader Howard

Cher
Photo courtesy: Fotos International / Archive Photos
Photo by: Bob Scott

Chi Chi LaRue
Photo by: Ed Karvoski, Jr.

The Rocky Horror Picture Show
Photo courtesy: Fotos International / Archive Photos

Dirk Shafer and Phil Donahue
Photo courtesy: Seventh Art Releasing
© Seventh Art Releasing 1995

Paul Lynde
Photo courtesy: Fotos International / Archive Photos

Anne Heche and Ellen DeGeneres
Photo courtesy: Archive Photos
Photo by: Reuters/ Fred Ser

Ed Karvoski, Jr.
Photo by: Jay Chun

Author's Acknowledgments

I would like to express my gratitude to my literary agent, Alison Picard, and my editor, John Scognamiglio, both for saying yes and for offering helpful guidance.

Many thanks to the magazine and newspaper editors who have most recently included my column and/or entertainment articles in their publications, including June Holloway at *Alabama Forum,* Darren Kissinger at *Baltimore Gay Paper,* Rudy Kikel at *Bay Windows,* Dennis Vercher at *Dallas Voice,* Monica Trasandes at *Frontiers,* French Wall at *The Guide,* Greg Montoya at *Out Front Colorado,* Tracy Baim at *Outlines,* Debbi Memoli at *Our Quarterly,* Tom Dyer at *Watermark,* and Doug Janousek and Bill Watson at *The Weekly News.*

And thanks to you, the readers. I urge you to continue to support gay-and-lesbian-friendly publishing and entertainment.

About the Author

As a comedy writer, Ed Karvoski, Jr. has written for Jay Leno and radio DJs at CBS, NBC, and the BBC. As an entertainment journalist, his work has appeared in national publications including *The Advocate, Out,* and *Poz,* as well as numerous regional publications from coast to coast. Karvoski is also the author of *A Funny Time to Be Gay* (Fireside/Simon & Schuster).